Sign Posts on the Christian Way

Sign Posts on the Christian Way
A Guide to the Devotional Life

BY PATRICK HANKEY

Dean of Ely Cathedral

Charles Scribner's Sons
New York

Preface

Now that the writing of this book is finished I find that it reminds me of one I used to read as a child. It was called *Madame How and Lady Why,* and was to be found in most children's nurseries in those days. The subject matter was widely different from mine for it concerned itself with such natural phenomena as why stars glitter, and how worms worm. But, like that very informative work, my own is concerned also with the how and the why. This book is in fact a modest attempt to explain the practices of the Christian religion and to show how they should be done; and it also tries to show why they are important and where they fit in to the great work of finding our way to God, or rather of responding to His guidance. We need to be persuaded that something matters if we are to work seriously to master its performance. In Sunday schools, Church schools and at home children often receive the elementary lessons in this subject, but it is to be feared that in many cases that early in-struction has to last them the rest of their lives. These chapters set out to provide the instruction which Christians need when childhood is over if they are to be grown-up spiritually as they are physically and mentally.

If a prospective reader glances at the list of chapter headings he will observe that some subjects, such as meditation, are dealt with at some length, while others have perhaps only a few pages. Length of treatment has nothing to do with the importance of the theme. It only means that it takes longer to deal with some subjects than with others.

Lastly I take this opportunity to acknowledge my debt to the General Theological Seminary in New York. By inviting me some years ago to give a course of lectures on ascetical theology the Seminary roused in me the desire to write this book, and has also given me many treasured friendships in the United States.

P.H.

Ely, Cambridgeshire,
England

Table of Contents

1. The Beginning of the Way

When, in 1940, Germany invaded France and prepared to follow up this victory by invading England
also, one of the precautions taken by the English
Government was to remove every sign post from the
roads. An enemy landing from the air or by sea
must be deprived of the considerable assistance they
would afford. The result was that the English also,
when they used the roads outside their own area,
found it very difficult to find their way about the
countryside. Every crossroad set them guessing.

There are many Christians nowadays who sin-
cerely want to travel the road from their present
selves to that destination which God desires them
to come to—to Heaven itself, in fact. Naturally they
want to know when they are on the right road as
they journey, and to have the wrong turnings clearly
marked, but it seems to them that the way to their
end is without sign posts; so they do not know how
to set about their task. There are, in fact, plenty
of sign posts to help them on their way, for the
Church has stored up a great deal of knowledge
about this. But they do not know of their existence.

For there is a branch of Christian theology
which is wholly concerned with this very matter.
Its content is this accumulated experience of the

Church, gathered from many people and places in the centuries of its life, as to the ways and means by which we learn the great lesson of our life. And that lesson is to learn to express within ourselves, with the help of divine grace, the image of Christ by the practice of the Christian virtues; and that we learn further how we may best apply the means given to us for overcoming the obstacles which lie in our path. In short, its business is to show us the best road and help us to keep to it.

It is with this subject that this book is concerned, namely the means which God has given us for living a life of interior union with Him. It is called Ascetical Theology, a term which sounds perhaps somewhat gloomy and forbidding, calling up pictures of emaciated bodies. But the nature of the road which leads to God Himself and the help He affords in travelling it can hardly be described as gloomy.

When people realize that God is moving them strongly to take to the road and to grow in grace, it sometimes happens that their only idea of responding to this experience is to do something more about their prayers and their church-going. But these, important though they are, will not by themselves provide what they need. They cannot be isolated from the other practices of Christian life. There are some very great books on prayer but they all assume that their readers have already laid certain foundations and have undertaken what the author of *The Imitation of Christ* called "the zeal-ous amendment of our *whole* life." Unless that con-dition is fulfilled these great books are incompre-hensible—and possibly even dangerous. The reader who seeks to plunge straight into this subject finds himself out of his depth before he reaches the second chapter and leaves the book in dejection. While, therefore, considerable space is devoted to prayer in this book, an attempt is made to relate that activity to the other activities of the Christian life, having regard to the purposes of God and to the end of man. In that setting alone can the nature and purpose of prayer be made clear.

So it will be found that what is said here on this great subject of prayer is of a simple kind and is designed to help that great army of Christians who feel its heights and depths are beyond them—that they are only at the beginning of its under-standing. And this teaching is preceded by some chapters of which the object is to help the reader to lay his foundations truly.

From the very beginning the Church has taught that the supreme need of all her children is that they should seek after a life of the highest interior union with God. That is the theme of the Scriptures from their opening picture of unfallen man walking and talking happily with God in Eden during the cool of the day, right through to their closing chap-ters in the Book of the Revelation. This is man's prerogative, that he should know the joy of union with God. Scupoli, in his *Spiritual Combat*, (the only book on the interior life which has powerfully affected Christians both in western and in eastern Christendom) expressed this truth in these emphatic words: "I will tell you plainly:—the greatest and most perfect thing a man may desire to attain to is to come near to God and dwell in union with Him."

When we think of it we realise that the Being of God Himself teaches us that man's interior life is of vital significance, and that in neglecting it, in leaving it as an undeveloped territory, man is denying himself that joy for which he was created, and for which he was redeemed. For although in this world God is known to us most intimately through what He has done, and is even now doing, on our planet—that is, in His activities of creation, redemption and sanctification—the most intense plane of His life is that unimaginable activity of love in which we are already included, and in which we are called upon to play our part.

We must clearly start with God Himself, and with His purposes for us. The perils of having self-perfection as one's aim in life—of trying to be perfect for one's own satisfaction—are always near. To attempt to provide a technique for spiritual self-improvement would be a wicked undertaking. We must clearly understand that everything begins and ends in Him, in that God "from whom all holy desires, all good counsels and all just works do proceed." The initiative lies always with Him, and

4

what we undertake must be a response to His love, deriving its urgency from our desire that He may have what He wants. I have said that we must clearly understand this, but it may well be that we find these truths difficult to understand at first; in that case we must make an act of faith, that is to say, we must accept as true what we do not fully understand.

And we must also begin with some thought about the end, that estate of life, towards which we would be moving. This is something that the Church has long realised to be a duty—to start with the end. We cannot consider the problem of *how to get to* a place until we have decided exactly what place it is we aim to reach; only then can we know in which direction to be moving. And, further, as when we are going to some place for a holiday we consider the sort of life we shall live when we get there so that we may take with us what we shall need, so also we must know everything that can be known about what we shall need at the end of this spiritual journey. The Lord Himself described with precision the principal contents of the luggage when He said, "Thou shalt love the Lord thy God with all thy heart and soul and strength and mind, and thy neighbour as thyself." We could hardly hope to be happy with God, and in the company of the blessed, unless we had learned already, during our years in this present life, something about this twofold love.

That initial difficulty was perceived by John

Bunyan who, in these matters, was a learned and experienced person. Here is his famous description of the setting forth of Pilgrim on that same journey with which we are concerned. (If you have not read, or do not remember, *Pilgrim's Progress* you should read it, as you travel the same path as Pilgrim).

"I dreamed, and behold I saw a man clothed with rags, standing in a certain place, with his face from his own house, a book in his hand and a great burden upon his back. I looked and saw him open the book and read therein, and as he read he wept and trembled and he brake out with a lament-able cry, saying 'What shall I do?' And I saw also that he looked this way and that way, as if he would run: yet he stood still because, as I perceived, he could not tell which way to go." And then the man, Evangelist, comes to this bewildered pilgrim and listens to the tale of his misery. At the end Evangelist asks him a question. "Do you see", he says, "yon wicket gate?" Pilgrim strains his eyes in the direction in which the other points, but at last he has to say "No." Then Evangelist says "Do you see yonder shining light?" And to that Pilgrim can only answer "I *think* I do."[1]

It brings to one's mind the word of the Lord about the power of a faith no larger than a mustard seed. It was enough to set Pilgrim on his way, and it will serve us in a like manner.

[1] From chap. 1.

2. The Christian Road

When people are making New Year resolutions, or a Lent rule, it sometimes happens that they address themselves in some such way as this: "I must not be so lazy in the morning," or "I must be a bit better tempered, or more self-controlled about smoking or eating." They then proceed to make a rule the purpose of which is that they will be rather more this, or rather less that. That does not sound a very interesting occupation, and one could hardly expect much fruit from it. It is rather as though the goal before us in life was that we should attain a moderate love, a discreet and temperate affection, even for God.

It is not in such terms that Our Lord has taught us. The prayer He has put into our mouths goes like this: "O my God, I desire to love Thee with all my heart, with all my mind, with all my soul and with all my strength, because Thou alone art perfectly good and worthy of love. Teach me to love Thee more and to love my neighbour as myself." There is an 'all or nothing' note in that which stirs our sluggish inclinations: it is a goal worth aiming at. But we must note what that goal is: it is perfection. It is to possess that aim in life which Christ expressly set before us when He said "Be ye perfect as your Father in Heaven is perfect." We may set ourselves to attain that end by contending now against this obstacle or that, by seeking now this virtue and now that, but we are not going to attain it by being moderate, any more than an athlete will get his honours by being moderate in his efforts. And we must not merely entertain a pious hope that somehow we shall reach that goal, but, like the saints, we must take practical steps to get there. The soul that eagerly responds to the infinitely tender interior movements of the Lord in the heart is going to know something of the utter joy of worshipping God in complete self-abandonment, without reservation of any kind. The distance between our present selves and that perfection is not to be reckoned in time. It is determined by the mighty Grace of God, and by our own steadfast resolution to respond to it.

But now, in what does this perfection consist? We cannot get any further if we have not a clear idea of that. The perfection of anything consists in becoming that for which it was specially made. Every creature has its own perfection. My eye would be perfect if it saw every object with perfect distinctness; my ear if it distinguished sounds in the same way, for that is what God made them for. But in what does the perfection of my whole person consist? The answer must depend on what we think we were made for. As Christians we believe— though our lives hardly bear witness to this—that we were made for God, and to enter ultimately into uninterrupted communion with Him. What is there, though, that could so unite me to my last end, to God Himself? If we knew that we should know in what our perfection consists.

We do really know the answer to that question; we have learnt it from our everyday experience. We are, we find, cut off from the people we do not like, we are united in some measure with those we do like. At a higher level we find that we are cut off from people when we are not desiring that good may befall them, and are united with them when we do so desire. It is this that we mean by being "in charity" with people—the first stage of it anyway. Unless we have enough charity in our hearts to achieve that modest desire we cannot even begin to have that understanding of them which any fellowship requires.

In no other terms can we hope for fellowship with God. Like can only hold communion with like, and God is love. We do not, indeed, generally speak of being in charity with God, but that phrase may more nearly than any other express the truth at the beginning anyway. We can return to that point, and use the word for the present. If my perfection will consist in communion with God, and if love is the means by which that communion can be brought about, the substance of Christian perfection is love. And this is precisely what the Scriptures tell us. "He that dwelleth in love dwelleth in God,

9

and God in him."[1] And again, "Above all these
things put on charity, which is the bond of perfect-
ness."[2] When we understand this truth so many
others, some of which sound rather harsh in our
ears, begin to become clear: as when the Lord says,
that "Whosoever shall seek to save his life shall
lose it; and whosoever shall lose his life shall preserve it."[3] There is a sentence in a prayer of
Charles de Foucauld which expresses this: "It is a
necessity of my love that I give myself into Thy
hands." For the effect of love is to make us forget
about ourselves and what we want; it makes us
think only of giving and finds its happiness there.

To return to the question of loving God; in
some forms for the examination of conscience based
on the Ten Commandments it is suggested that
we ask ourselves, "Have I loved God as much as I
ought?" This might lead one to think that there is a
correct amount of love to be expended on Him. It
rarely happens that one finds later the question
"Have I loved my parents as much as I ought?" At
that point the good sense of the Fifth Command-
ment prevents such a mistake. "Honour" is a safe
and adequate word in that case, and would not
"allegiance" or "loyalty" be best when we think
of God? We love God by the willingness, loyalty
and resolution of our service to Him: we are in

1 1 John 4.16.
2 Col. 3.14.
3 Luke 17.33.

10

charity with God by the cheerfulness of our acceptance of all the circumstances of our life.

Here are some admirable sentences from St.
Thomas Aquinas on this point. "He who wills to
enjoy the gift of loving is perfect when he loves as
much as he is able. For then the whole heart of man
is borne towards God, and this is the perfection of
the love of heaven, unattainable here by reason
of life's infirmities which do not allow us to meditate
upon God all the time. So too, by loving, a man
may strive to keep himself free for God and things
divine, putting other matters aside, save as life's
needs require, and this is the perfection of love
possible in this life, yet not for all who love. Then
too there is the way of loving which consists in
habitually setting one's heart on God, so that one
thinks and wills nothing contrary to divine love,
and this grace is common to all who love."[4] That
is a subject on which St. Thomas more than most
had the right to speak. He was a great lover of God.

The aim of our spiritual training, then, is
that we may come to have a perfect devotion to
God only. It is essential that this devotion be given
to Him alone because He alone is a perfect object
for such a devotion; "for thou only art holy" as the
Gloria in excelsis declares. To be completely devoted
to anyone else, or anything else—any cause, however good—is seen by us at once to be a fault, and a
dangerous fault. We notice that the words we use

[4] *Summa* II. ii Q.xxiv, Art. 8.

to describe utter devotion to imperfect objects are always critical, such words as fanatical, for instance, and uxorious.

The most subtle, and therefore the most dangerous, of such imperfect objects of devotion is self-perfection, or, as it might be described, devotion for the sake of devotion. Self-perfection is often made, consciously or unconsciously, the supreme object of human devotion. In popular religious literature, as well as in more ambitious treatises, we hear much of "the vital importance of character building," the "imperative duty of self-culture," of "self-development," or of "realising our personalities." "Love is the great thing" it is said (quite rightly), "and therefore (quite wrongly) our chief aim is to learn to be loving." All these phrases imply the ideal of self-perfection."[5]

It is serious-minded and even religious people who are likely to fall into this dangerous error, and this may well be the explanation of the uncomfortable fact that the unserious are so often nicer, and indeed better, people than many who are deeply in earnest. For the truth may be that the latter are in earnest about themselves rather than about God. Their behaviour towards others may be indistinguishable from that of a truly good man and yet be quite unloving, for while they help their neighbour in some difficulty, they do not do so for the simple reason that the other needs their help, but

[5] A. D. Kelly, *Values of the Christian Life,* pp. 33-37.

rather they think of their neighbour as someone who affords them an opportunity of being kind, for the cultivation of that virtue in themselves. The real aim of their action is their own perfection, which they are seeking for their own satisfaction.

We are, then, to aim at nothing less than perfection—the Lord made that quite clear—but we are not to make that perfection an end in itself. It is because God is, and because He is what He is, that we strive to "eschew evil and do good" altogether, so that we may know and love Him better. God cannot be used for the purpose of perfecting our character.[6] Knowing that we belong to God we can then safely pray Him that we may have an undying zeal for our own perfection, for it will be the perfection of one of His possessions; the urge to do this comes then from our growing love of Him who loves us. We shall be striving for perfection in ourselves to give Him joy.

The first thing that God gives us for our journey towards perfection is the desire for it. For there is such a desire. We may not want it very strongly or constantly, and there is, as we have just seen, a danger that we may want it for our own purposes, but we do want it. And God has put this desire into our hearts in order that it may help us to draw near to Him.

Having this God-given desire, what we need to

[6] See St. Francis de Sales, *The Devout Life,* chap. 1 for a description of true devotion.

13

know is this. When we say, "O my God I desire to love Thee," how can we make that desire pure and strong, and therefore more moving and controlling? We need, in fact, something that we can do about this, some practice which can help it to come to pass. Now, of course, any true prayer is practice in this activity, but it would help us if we could do something which was specifically directed to that end.

There is a godly habit which we can form and which can help to keep an edge on this aspiration. It is the habit of starting each day afresh, as though we had never made a beginning before. It is as though we said to ourselves, "whatever I may have done yesterday, and the day before, to-day, anyway, I am going to make a beginning. O my God, I purpose firmly to-day, at least for the next twenty-four hours, to set my feet to follow the path of perfection by the Grace of the Holy Spirit." The limitation in time is very important. There is a much better chance that we shall do something effective about one day than about a week or more. We are in fact going to renew that undertaking next morning, but that will be a new promise: at the moment there is only one day to deal with. It is, indeed, only when circumstances make lifelong promises unavoidable, as in marriage or in ordination, that such long-term promises are excusable,

This is not, of course, novel advice. It has been well tried for many centuries: there is something of this, surely, in that "renewing of your mind" that the Apostle speaks about. And here is this same advice on the lips of the great hermit St. Antony. As he lay dying the hermits of the desert, his spiritual children, came from all parts to be with him at his end, and to receive his last counsels. "My children", he said to them, "I am going the way my fathers have gone before me. God is calling me to Him and I myself yearn to be among the heavenly choirs. My dear ones, waste not in a moment the labours you have undergone during so many years; and lest you may, imagine to yourselves that each day of your life is the first in which you enter upon the career of perfection."[7]

If we form the habit of starting each day with some act of that kind (which can be performed while one is dressing, or on the way to work) there is much less chance that we shall think that there is plenty of time. It keeps an edge on our resolution, helps to rekindle daily our desire, and it is, as we say, good practice.

[7] *Vita. S. Antoni,* par. 91.

3. Purity of Intention

When Jeremy Taylor was planning the great book in which he tried to set out the whole duty of a Christian—the book he names *Holy Living and Dying*—he decided to begin it with what he describes as "the general instruments and means serving to a holy life." Of these means he chooses three as having paramount importance. The first is "care of our time," a subject to which we shall give attention at a later stage. The second is "purity of intention." The third is "the practice of the presence of God," which will be considered in Chapter 8.

Almost at once he gives examples of the importance of that second instrument, purity of intention. "For he that prays out of custom, or gives alms for praise, or fasts to be accounted religious, is but a Pharisee in his devotion, and a beggar in his alms, and a hypocrite in his fast. But a holy end sanctifies all these and other actions which can be made holy, and gives distinction to them, and procures acceptance. For as to know the end distinguishes a man from a beast, so to choose a good end distinguishes him from an evil man."[1] He requires in fact, as the Gospels do, that we question ourselves about our

[1] *Holy Living,* chap. I, sect. 2.

16

activities, asking ourselves our reason for doing them, why we are taking pains over this, or taking little trouble over that, and for whom we are doing this. "If a man visits his sick friend and watches at his pillow for charity's sake and because of his old affection, we approve it; but if he does it in hope of a legacy, he is a vulture, and only watches for the carcass. The same things are honest and dishonest: the manner of doing them and the end of the design makes the separation".[2]

We have good reason to suppose, and often observe, that our intention is impure, that is to say that there is more than one ingredient in it, a mixed motive. This is indeed disturbing, but the fact that we have perceived the mixture, and that we are not deceived about the purity of our motive, is extremely important. We are far less likely to come to grave harm if we recognise clearly the strength of our self-love and how powerfully we are being affected by it. It is blindness in this matter which is so dangerous.

Taylor drew up a list of "signs of purity of intention" because he realised that "many cases may happen in which a man's heart may deceive him, and he may not well know what is in his own spirit."[3] He observes first that when we are cheerful and prompt over our work and play but become sluggish when engaged in any religious practice, there

[2] *Ibid.*
[3] *Ibid.*

is clearly something wrong. He might have added that our intention is also impure if we are cheerful and prompt in religious practices because religion happens to be our hobby. Then there are all those impurities which creep in because our attention is largely concentrated on the good opinion or the censure of our neighbours; our desire for their good opinion becomes entangled in our readiness to serve God. Or we may discover that, while we are normally easy and good-natured in society, we are often morose and silent at home. Further we shall realise that we do not love what is good for its own sake if we are not glad whenever and wherever we see goodness. We must rejoice to hear that people who do not like us are doing good.

Very closely connected with this subject of purity of intention is that of purity of conscience. Each of these affects every part of our life, and each is of vital importance when we approach God in prayer. A pure conscience does not, of course, mean that we never do anything wrong. As St. James says in his matter-of-fact way "in many things we all stumble." It means, first, that we are steadily resolved not to keep anything back, to have nothing of which we say "I am going on doing that although I know it is wrong. I cannot do without it," or "I cannot believe it matters much." Such an attitude is fatal. Secondly it means that we do all we can to make our penitence as complete as possible when we have yielded to temptation, however

habitual that sin has become. Here are some sentences from Père Grou's description of the perfect
man which admirably define the meaning of a pure
conscience. "He has made a determination once for
all to refuse nothing to God, to grant nothing to
self-love, and never to commit a voluntary fault."
We may find that beginning rather obvious, and
depressing. He goes on, however, "but he does not
perplex himself: he goes on courageously: he is
not too particular. If he falls into a fault, he does
not agitate himself: he humbles himself at the sight
of his own weakness: he raises himself up and
thinks no more about it. If he were to fall a hundred
times a day he would not despair: but he would
stretch out his hands lovingly to God and beg Him
to lift him up and take pity on him." The soul that
is really turned to God is full of sorrow for sin
and of distress for its consequences, and yet it has,
as Grou here observes, an equanimity and steadiness.
The reason for this is that if we do not turn a blind
eye towards our sins and explain them away, but
confess them with sorrow as sins, we are forgiven.
Forgiveness does not by any means take away the
pain of remembered sins; it may very well increase
it. But when we are forgiven such charity pours
into our hearts that the burden becomes light and
invigorating.

There is nothing that can more surely destroy,
or at least gravely impair the first movements of
charity in a heart than an impure conscience. For a

while the child of God may have held firmly that nothing but the best is good enough for Him. Then it can happen that he gradually begins to make concessions to his various appetites, to let himself off this or that: the general standard is lowered and the conscience ceases to reprove him for these concessions. Something a good deal less than the best becomes good enough until the soul awakes to the fact that it no longer cares about the service of God: it is without interest and it is burdensome.

The truth is that the yoke of which Jesus spoke is not easy and the burden is not at all light when the conscience has become impure and, as a consequence, the charity of God has left the heart. Thomas à Kempis says "If there be joy in the world, certainly the man whose heart is pure possesses it."[4] It is a dreary occupation to serve God half-heartedly. We might well desire to have a pure conscience for our own sakes; we must try to want it for God's sake.

[4] *Imitation of Christ*, Bk. II, chap. 4.

4. The Examined Life

The value of the gift so earnestly desired by Robert Burns, that we may "see ourselves as others see us" will depend on the discrimination of our friends. For those surrounded by foolish admirers it is a menace. But if our desire is that we should see ourselves as God sees us, we shall probably need some apparatus in our daily life which provides the means of learning this lesson. That is what the practice of self-examination is. There is a passage in *The Imitation of Christ* which indicates clearly its importance.

"There is but little light in us, and this we quickly lose through negligence. Often times too we do not perceive our inward blindness, how great it is. We often do ill, and do worse in excusing it. We are sometimes moved with passion, and we mistake it for zeal. We blame little things in others, and pass over greater offences in ourselves. We are quick enough in perceiving and weighing what we suffer from others, but we heed not what others suffer from us."[1]

It is of course true that one of the ordinary results of our life of prayer will be the enlightening of our conscience. The more we come to know

[1] Book II, chap. 5.

21

God, the more we learn about ourselves; and this is especially true when the prayer is being constantly nourished by the Gospels, as it should be. As we contemplate His perfection we learn with greater precision the particular ways in which we are failing to follow Him. To know God is to know self and our prayers are helping us to know Him.

Self-scrutiny is therefore a continued process inseparably bound up with growth in grace "and in the knowledge and love of our Lord Jesus Christ." None the less it is generally true that it is best to have definite moments in our lives when we examine our consciences, such as a brief review of each day during our night prayers, a more detailed scrutiny before receiving Holy Communion (remembering how St. Paul says "let a man examine himself, and so let him eat of that bread, and drink of that cup"),[2] and at longer intervals a careful examina-tion which may or may not be before sacramental confession.

It is sometimes said that such a practice of self-examination is not only unnecessary but may actually do harm by inducing a condition of scrup-ulosity about details. It is clear, of course, that if a person suffers from this moral disease very different advice should be given him in this matter. There appears to be more weight of objection in the remark of the Abbé de Tourville: "Christian teachers ask a soul to look at itself only when it requires

[2] 1 Cor. 11.28.

22

to be brought low, to be humiliated and frightened, sobered in its view of itself and of the world."[3] But probably most of us would agree that we need that treatment rather often. Anyway, self-scrutiny does not seek to produce gloomy introverts: its result is rather a disentangling of our confused aspirations and motives so that "forgetting those things which are behind, and reaching forth unto those things which are before, I press toward the mark for the prize of the high calling of God in Christ Jesus."[4] The Christian cannot afford time and energy for pessimistic brooding over past failures: but he will do well to provide stated times in his life for that disentangling.

As to the daily examination of conscience during our night prayers, it is important that we realise the limitations of that practice. It is improbable that we learn much of importance about ourselves in this way because the period under scrutiny is too brief. One day is usually very much like another day; the difficulties and temptations of Monday are almost the same as those of Tuesday and Wednesday. It is therefore likely that there will be little difference in the sins for which we must seek God's pardon. But although there is this humiliating sameness about these daily confessions they are nevertheless important and we should suffer loss if they ceased. It does matter that we

[3] *Letters of Direction*, p. 69.
[4] Phil. 3.13.

own up daily, and daily renew our purpose of amendment. These scrutinies should, however, be brief unless the past day has been exceptional in any way, in which case we should be more careful since new circumstances may be revealing.

The self-examination which can do much more for the increase of our self-knowledge is that which is made by one preparing for sacramental confession or by one who has the valuable private rule of making such a scrutiny, say, once a quarter or at longer intervals. Looking back over this more extended period of time they are much better able to observe the dominant disposition of their soul—what it is that is really urging them to do this or refrain from that. Another thing that will stand out then with some clarity is the general movement of their life, in what ways they are growing—or not growing—towards what goal they are directing themselves. We should attach a high importance to this practice if we want to lead an examined life.

As to the method we use, each will have to find out by experiment what works best for him: the following are only general suggestions some of which may be found of use.

We begin by trying not to think about ourselves at all, or our neighbour: we pray to God, "in thy light shall we see light." If we have been speaking to Him we shall be less inclined to think of other standards of conduct than His, nor shall we slip into the sterile consideration of the ways in which we have broken the rules. When we have prayed a while it may be best to think quite generally of the time that has elapsed since we last made this examination, where we have been and what our main occupations were, noting especially anything out of the ordinary that has happened—not any sins out of the ordinary, but any events. If we have been brought into contact with some new person or work, or have had a holiday or an illness and so forth, we may well examine ourselves in relation to that change first of all. As this may well be the most revealing as well as exacting part of the exercise it is well to do it while we are fresh. After that we may turn to routine, the ordinary occupations and usual difficulties. We are painfully familiar with them; some of them we meet almost every day in our examination of conscience; they are old enemies. But we must not be unreasonably perturbed because we come across them so often. As long as the circumstances of our life remain the same—meeting the same people, doing the same job—its difficulties will remain the same and its temptations. We may think that we should do better against a new set of circumstances but if we are to judge by what is happening in us now we should conclude that new conditions would only mean new sins, and it is difficult to see any advantage in that. We must believe that God has chosen our battle ground wisely for us and look to see what progress we are making in dealing with these present difficulties. It is unreasonable for us to say "It is no good for me to go on confessing my sins for I always seem to say the same thing?"

In making this examination it is important that we should be as concrete as possible. If we want to grow spiritually we must not be vague in our accusation against ourselves. We shall not be content to note that we have been proud, for instance, but observe the particular ways and circumstances in which we have sinned against humility. If we know at what points our pride breaks out we may be more watchful in future, like a dog at a rat hole. Anyway, it is our sins we want to tell God about, not our general state of sinfulness. Perhaps the most difficult part of this "examination of conscience" relates to the things we have left undone, our sins of omission. There is some uncertainty about determining what we could have done and what we are blameworthy for not having done when we look back after any passage of time. It is advisable to be as concrete and clear as possible in this, careful not to accuse ourselves unfairly. But these sins of omission must somehow be reviewed so that our purpose of amendment may be applied to their remedy and not remain a vague resolve to do better.

Most of us know well enough that evil cannot be eliminated from the soul by a single act of repentance. "We cannot be perfect in a day," said St. Teresa. When we tend to be depressed because we seem to make so little observable prog-

ress it is well to remember an incident in *Alice
through the Looking Glass*. The Red Queen, taking
Alice by the hand, made her run faster and faster
until they both collapsed panting under the same
tree from which they had started. "Here you see,"
explained the Queen, "it takes all the running we
can do to keep in the same place." In the life of
the spirit it often does take all the running we
can do to keep in the same place. The important
thing is that we should not give way to despondency.
We should consider the present circumstances of
our life and make sure that we are not running over
ground which has for some reason beyond our
control become exceptionally heavy, or to use
another metaphor, rowing against a tide which is
running fast against us. St. Francis de Sales said,
"Let us not be troubled because of our imperfec-
tions, for our perfection consists in fighting against
them, and we cannot fight them unless we see
them or conquer them unless we meet them."[5]
Our resolution to avoid sin must not be shaken by
the fact that we so often fail to keep it. It is like
"standing orders" framed and glazed and hung
up in the council chamber of our soul. Standing
orders get violated, but they are still "standing
orders." Julian of Norwich wrote, "Our courteous
Lord willeth not that his servants despair . . . for
our falling hindereth Him not in loving us."[6]

Here is some advice on the means by which

[5] From *Introd. to the Devout Life*, Pt. I, chap. 5.
[6] *Revelations of Divine Love*, chap. 39.

we may lead an examined life given by Tissot in his *Interior Life*[7] which indicates the underlying purpose of the practices we have been considering. "When the water spouts forth in profusion from the host of little holes in the rose of a watering pot, would it not be a tedious and troublesome matter to shut off each little hole one after another in order to cut off the flow? And if there were a tap lower down, enabling one to stop the flow by a single turn, would it not be stupid to tire oneself with trying to stop all the little holes? And that all the more because there is always a risk of their coming open again. He whose examination of conscience stops at details and outward things is passing his time in stopping up the little holes. The inward glance turns the tap. To stop at details and at what is outward is to remain at the circumference and to manoeuvre on the surface of the soul. I go straight to the centre and take possession of my whole soul, when I cast this penetrating glance at my dominant disposition."

Tissot makes this action sound like a convenient and easy short cut. It is of course nothing of the kind. That is clearly true about the dominant disposition; it is this which is really controlling us, impelling us to do this or to refuse to do that. We can sometimes discover its nature by stopping in the middle of some activity and questioning ourselves as to why, for instance, we are taking a

[7] Page 300.

great deal of trouble over this or doing the other carelessly. But it is generally true that we shall not have the knowledge we need for casting the penetrating glance beneath our surface unless we have humbly practiced the elementary lessons which lead to the living of an examined life.

As we have seen we must be penitent if we are to serve God with a pure conscience. This is the first command laid on us in the Gospels, "Repent ye;" and our Lord tells us with dreadful clearness what will befall those who refuse to obey, "Except ye repent, ye shall all likewise perish."[8] It is a teaching which we accept without question even in our immaturity. If there is doubtfulness in our minds it is connected with the manner in which we are to do this and not with the need to repent. It is of great importance that our thoughts on this point should be as clear and concrete as possible.

The inclination is to think of repentance as being something that one feels, and it would be absurd to deny that our feelings have a part in it. But it is wise to regard repentance as being primarily something that we do, an activity. Our response to conviction of sin, and the call to repent, is to be like that of the multitudes who listened to the Baptist preaching about them. "And the people asked him, saying, What shall we do then?"[9] And

[8] Luke 13.3.
[9] Luke 3.10.

it is something they can do that the penitent souls have always rightly desired.

The traditional answer to their question and to ours is that three activities are to be discerned in repentance, contrition, confession and amendment. It may help us to be clear and concrete if we deal with this vital subject under these heads.

CONTRITION

It is at this point that it is essential for us to realise that while a feeling of sadness is a great help, it is not in itself contrition. St. Paul underlines this distinction: "I rejoice", he wrote, "not that ye were made sorry, but that ye sorried to re- pentance . . . For godly sorrow worketh repentance unto salvation: but the sorrow of the world worketh death."[10] It is clear from this, and from other passages in the Scriptures, that the con- trition which plays the initial part in the salva- tion of each of us is rooted in some knowledge of God and in our true understanding of our relation- ship to Him. The fruitless sorrow of which St. Paul spoke is that feeling of regret and pain which arises out of our wounded self-love. The child can understand that if some fault of his had never been exposed he might never have experienced any sorrow for its commission. The adult knows that when he has done something he is ashamed of, he is not only sorry because what he has done is wrong;

[10] 2 Cor. 7.9-10.

in part at least (perhaps mostly) he is sorry because he does not like the feeling of being ashamed of himself. These truths are familiar to most of us, but it does not follow that we shall be spiritually alert enough to examine ourselves about them. A great writer on the spiritual life, after noting that even children know that it is no good to admit one's fault if one is not sorry for the people one has injured, goes on: "But since this is a truth which is as seldom practised as it is generally known, it will not be superfluous to call the attention of the reader to it."[11] The truth is that contrition and remorse, or attrition, produce the same feeling, which shows how dangerous it is to think only in terms of "feeling." As we have already seen, contrition is grounded not only in some knowledge of God, "seeing our sins in the light of God's countenance" as the Psalmist says, but also in our understanding of our relationship to Him. This understanding is a part of the foundation on which our spiritual life must be built if our religion is not to do us more harm than good. St. Thomas Aquinas defines contrition as that which arises from "filial fear" when we fall into sin. Sin is then something that has happened to that father-son relationship, and something, therefore, that can have disastrous consequences for our whole family life, that is, in relation to God our Father, and our brother and sister in Christ. He defines attrition as

[11] Scaramelli, *Directorum Asceticum*.

the result of "servile fear"—the fear of someone without family rights and responsibilities, who must just do as he is told for fear of being punished.

But for the purpose of examining the nature of our sorrow for sin the distinction which may well prove most valuable is between the sadness which results from our love of the person we have wronged, God Himself, our neighbour, and ourselves as being beloved by God, and, on the other hand, the sadness which results from love of ourselves, and the regret at the loss of the good opinion of others and of ourselves. People are sometimes gravely perturbed because they seem to have so little sorrow for sin. These should be, as far as possible, re-assured. In the end, it is true, they must experience this sorrow; they are not, however, at the end but at the beginning. They must accept the fact that they have little or no feelings in this matter as yet, but they can require of themselves a change of will and of conduct.

CONFESSION

It is at this point in repentance that the soul receives so much help through being given something to *do,* something which is wholly relevant to the situation. It is not enough that we admit in a general way that we are sinners. It is necessary that we say, "I am one who is guilty of these sins of thought, word, deed and omission" with full acceptance of our responsibility for these acts and omissions. It is not only our sinfulness that we confess but our sins, and if we are to do that we must, so far as possible, know what they are. In fact we have to make that self-examination we have just been considering.

This will sometimes seem to be quite unnecessary. It can happen that what has moved a soul to repentance is the pain, misery, shame or despair which has fallen on him because of some one grave sin, or habit of sin. That sin has come to loom so large in his life that it may well be darkening every corner of it, so that he has come to feel that if only he could deal with that everything else would be well. There are, however, many other sins in his life. Yet when he is told that he must look for these also, that it is his whole life, with its complex relationships with God and with man which he must examine, he may be impatient. Nevertheless he should do this. Even if it proves impossible for him at that juncture to take those other sins with full seriousness it is almost certain that later on, when his conscience has become more alert, he will wish that he had been better advised.

There are also those who, while recognising the emphasis of the Gospel on the need for repentance, yet do not find anything in their past or their present which greatly perturbs them. Their immunity from grave sin may well be due to sheltered conditions in their daily life: their comparatively venial sins might be more deadly if the shelter were

not there, or if opportunity came with its temptations. The help they may need at this moment is in
perceiving their sins of omission, which can have
such sad consequences for themselves and for others.
It must certainly help them if they come to realise
that their life *is* sheltered, and that they are required
to use this period for growth and not for repining
at their lot or for stagnation.

There is a passage somewhere in the writings
of Dom Marmion which deals with another possibility. "Why is it", he asks, "that a soul which has
got accustomed to say 'No' to the known will of
God in the matter of small sins, cannot hope to
preserve for any length of time the life of communion with God? Because," he answers, "these
faults coldly admitted, calmly committed, which
pass into accepted habit without the soul feeling
any contrition, inevitably result in a diminution
of teachableness, of vigilance, of our power of
resistance to temptation. Experience shows that,
from a deliberate negligence in little sins we slide
insensibly, but almost always fatally, into very
grave sins. I will go further than that. Let us
suppose a soul which seeks God with sincerity in
all things, loving Him truly, and it happens to such
a soul, through its weakness, to consent to a very
grave sin. That deadly sin is, for such a soul, an
immense misery, for it has broken the communion
with God. But that great fault, occurring as it were
all by itself, is far less dangerous to such a soul
than the venial faults of habit, done deliberately,

34

by that other person we have been thinking of, whose lesser faults are committed so lightly." It is clear why this is the case. If a person with a true and controlling love of God is overwhelmed by some great temptation, that event, being a thing most lamentable to that soul, becomes the starting point of an increase in humility, a new throwing of himself on God, a stimulus to love more generously, faithfully and watchfully. But in that second case, the fact that he is going on every day doing little things which he knows to be wrong, admitting them without true sorrow or any purpose of amendment, has produced in him a condition in which the supernatural action of God cannot operate. If we are continually saying "No" to God we cannot have the hardihood to suppose that we can go on living in communion with Him. For each of us the great task of our life is to learn to say "Yes" to Him always. Our self-examination is concerned with the times when we have said No.

It is the vital need for this confession which is so strongly emphasised by Our Lord in His story of the Prodigal Son. He makes it clear that the Prodigal did not return to his father in order to obtain forgiveness. It is expressly stated that he did not hope for that. "Father," he says, "I have sinned against heaven, and in thy sight, and am no more worthy to be called thy son: make me as one of thy hired servants."[12] That was the most he had hoped for. He came back from the far country

[12] Luke 15.

to make his confession. He allowed himself to hope only that, if his father would listen to that, he might be allowed to live somewhere near and to work for him. It is the Prodigal Son we should take as our pattern. If our approach to repentance is at all like his—concentrating on the need to confess what we have done—then we can believe that we have a godly sorrow for our sins.

AMENDMENT

When we have come to know this need to confess there is no difficulty about this third activity of a true repentance, for we shall be firm and honest in our purpose of amendment, willing to make any satisfaction we can for injuries we have done to others, and ready to take all possible steps to prevent the recurrence of those temptations. It is only those who are wholly moved by self-love who dare to commit sins because, as they believe, they can always repent and be forgiven, or will even confess to God sins which they do not purpose seriously to fight against. St. Gregory said, "he that mourneth over his sins yet continues to commit them, either does not know what repentance is, or else acts as if he does not know." Neither will there, with this disposition, be serious difficulty about those other conditions of penitence, humility and integrity. We shall know what has to be said and how it is to be said.

In general, we may all need to be reminded

that penitence should be—or should become—a "state"rather than an "act": that is, we must not rest content with being people who have repented but be striving to become penitents, after the manner of St. Peter and St. Mary Magdalen, whose penitence would be a permanent part of them. It is not enough that we turn away from sin from time to time. We have to learn as soon as we can what sin is by seeing it against the background of the love of God, and so hating it at every moment and realising our perpetual involvement in it. So a Christian community is one in which all the members find it hard to be censorious towards one another, since each is himself a penitent.

But being in a state of penitence does not mean the same as being in a state of continual worry or fear about our sins. We should not be at all happy about a child who showed signs of that when he had sinned against his parents. The penitent lives with the sins which the Lord has pardoned, and that is both his joy and his sorrow. There is no stage in his life here when to say "Lord have mercy upon me" does not come naturally to him and express the deepest conviction of his state and needs. Indeed, if our spiritual growth continues throughout life as we pray that it may, we shall become on the one hand more and more deeply penitent, and on the other, more moved to thanks-giving because of God's complete forgiveness.

5. Prayer

This matter of prayer, which has been so often the joy or the despair of Christian souls, is one on which it is particularly important that we go back to the beginning and try to look at it afresh. The question with which we ought to start is, surely, what is prayer for? If we are hazy on that point or in error it is certain that we shall perform this activity badly and with ill effects.

If we examine the prayer which we may well have been taught to offer as a small child we shall be led to assume that prayer is an acknowledgment that, as a child of God, we depend on Him, as we depend upon our parents; and also that it is an exercise of love for those whom our Heavenly Father has given to us to be our neighbours in life. "O God, bless my father and mother, my brother, sister and friends: and bless me and make me a good child, Amen." Having thus committed ourselves and our loved ones into His keeping we could hop into bed with a good conscience.

Clearly a part of the answer to our question, "What is prayer for?" lies there and continues to be found there throughout our lives. To kneel down and say slowly and with recollection "Father"—that is, by itself, a prayer within the great tradition of

38

Christian prayer. It is to hand oneself over to His keeping with the utmost confidence. And that prayer is even more deeply Christian when we say not only "My Father" but "Our Father", bringing those others in and behaving as though we loved our neighbours as much as we love ourselves. But if we were to find—as we well might do— that men and women in their thirties, fifties or even seventies, were still saying that prayer they learned at their mother's knee and nothing more, we should be disconcerted and distressed. For we know that prayer is something more than an accept-ance of our dependence upon God and something more than intercession, however important both these activities are.

The fact is that the answer to our question "What is prayer for?" is that it is not *for* anything. It is simply what happens when the soul which understands that it was created to praise, reverence and serve God our Lord and that its end lies in Him and not in itself, looks towards Him. It is something which occurs when we realise that the divine truths we are thinking about actually and at the moment *are*. Of course when we do a thing like that there are, as it were, by-products of our act, but we do not pray because prayer has by-products. We pray because we must.

For prayer is not a spiritual exercise compar-able in its purpose to physical exercises. We may do the latter in the morning with the object of keeping physically fit, and then get on with the work of the day. Now prayer does in fact help to keep us spiritually fit, but that is not what we do it for: that is what I have called a by-product. If we really thought along those lines we should remain in prayer what we so easily are when we are not praying, the centre of everything. Even God Himself would exist for our purposes.

When we understand that this is the true nature of prayer we shall not ask ourselves the question, "What is wrong with my prayers?" for we shall realise as we reflect on their poverty that what we have to ask is, "What is wrong with me?" The words of our prayer are good, the order in which we say them is good, and so are the time and place of their saying—at least as good as we can contrive. But my prayers come out of me, what is good in me will be good about my prayers: what is bad in me will be bad about my prayers. We shall all have discovered that directly there is any renewing of our mind or unburdening of our conscience there is immediately a difference in our prayers; they become at once livelier, stronger and more loving. We are reminded when we come to Holy Communion that we must be able to say that we truly and earnestly repent us of our sins, and are in love and charity with our neighbours and intend to lead a new life. We must also prepare ourselves for our daily prayers by trying to be such people. If these are not our resolute intentions our prayers will become more and more the expression of our ordinary self-seeking, self-loving selves—attempts to get God to give us what we cannot get for ourselves or even what we are too lazy to try to get for ourselves. The remote preparation for prayer is our daily striving for those virtues on which all else has to be built, humility, charity, fortitude and so forth. William Temple said somewhere in *Christus Veritas,* "Right relation between prayer and conduct is not that conduct is supremely important and prayer may help it, but that prayer is supremely important and conduct tests it."

The natural man lives, one might say, in the centre of a circle. He has ranged around him on the circumference of the circle the other objects which are real to him. There are, for instance, his loved ones, home, friends, job, pet recreations and enthusiasms, and there is also God (or rather, since it is really too difficult to get God Himself on to the circumference of any circle, there is, let us say, religion). If we bring this natural, self-centred self to prayer it goes on doing what it has been doing all day, sitting in the centre of its circle and turning from one part of the circumference to the other, drawing towards itself now this and now that. What we are called upon to do if we are to make Christian prayer is to step out of the centre of the circle—or at least try to do that—and to realise that God is the centre of everyone and everything, and that we are ourselves on the circumference of the circle with everyone and everything else.

This truth helps us to understand something which we might otherwise find disconcerting. Quite immature Christians are often better satisfied by their prayers than are those who, in the Christian sense, are more grown-up. The first prays easily with fervour; the latter often feels miserably cool and sluggish. This is very far indeed from meaning that the immature is praying better than the adult Christian; indeed the reverse is true. What is happening is that the natural forces, instincts, desires of the largely self-centred person are being poured into his prayers: his orisons are being warmed at the fire of his self-love which is fanned by the strength of his determination to get what he wants. The latter is trying to pray out of love for God, and to want only the things which God wants, because He wants them. That is difficult, and, not having advanced very far along the path whose perfect expression is Our Lord's prayer in the Garden of Gethsemane, he naturally finds that his prayers lack fervour. In fact, one of the first lessons for anyone who wants to make Christian prayer is to pay scant attention to its temperature. Quite un-Christian prayer may be made with extreme fervour. Many great saints have observed that they have passed through long periods of extreme aridity in prayer. This does not mean that when such dryness occurs it can be taken as a sign of progress, but that it is a mistake to pay too much attention to the thermometer. If we want to know how we are getting on—and it is excusable to want to know that—then we had better look at our wills rather than our feelings. "Thy will not mine, O Lord." It is the person who is trying to lead an unselfish life, dedicated to God and his neighbour, who begins to learn what prayer is. "Trying" is the significant word, for even our unsuccessful attempts to forget about ourselves have a reward beyond their apparent deserts.

When we realise the importance of being, or trying to be, the sort of person who can make Christian prayer we can understand what a writer meant when he said, "Prayer for Christianity is a continuous spiritual state, within which separate acts, indeed, find their place."[1] What we call "my prayers" are then the moments in the day when we consciously and deliberately express what is in our soul at all times, and by so doing we gradually form and support in us this state of prayer. There was a Carmelite nun, living of course in total seclusion from the world. Before she joined that community she had been accustomed to spend much time each day at her prayers; but when she became a nun she found, she said, that she had so little time for it. It was of course true that, in that busy life, the amount of time she could spend on her knees, giving her whole attention to God and offering

[1] A. L. Lilley, *Prayer and Christian Theology*, pp. 8, 9.

43

Him deliberately her worship and service was much restricted. But it was adequate because, as she worked, she was facing in the same direction as at her prayers. She was learning to live in a state of prayer, as Brother Lawrence has described in his *Practice of the Presence of God.* It is this coherence between the self that prays and the self when it is otherwise occupied which we must all seek. It is impossible to turn abruptly from a disorderly and careless life and to find oneself at once illuminated and strengthened in prayer. It cannot be treated as something we keep in drawers and take out at certain times and then put back again. Prayer comes out of *us,* and if there is something wrong with us, that same something will be wrong with our prayers.

So much for the remote preparation. The more immediate preparation, what we do when we are already on our knees but have not yet begun to pray, will be considered in chapter 8 on "The Practice of the Presence of God." There is only one point to be made here. In order to pray we must be aware not only of our own reality but of God's reality also. He must be real in the sense that He is not simply Someone who is somewhere, but Someone who is here, so close that He knows all and sees all. When we complain that we find prayer dull, or that our thoughts wander, or that we suffer from a sense of the futility of praying, it may be that our prayers have been a speaking to

Someone vague and shadowy—or even a mono‑
logue, a talking to ourselves, even though that self
is our best self. We must know God. At one time
I lived and worked in the heart of the city of
Westminster, a place more visited by tourists from
all over the world than any other in the British
Isles. One met them in the Abbey and the Houses
of Parliament: they "did" those places probably
more thoroughly than any of us who lived there
had ever done them. They could sometimes answer
questions about them which we could not answer.
But they did not *know* Westminster as we knew
it: they did not know the feel of it, and the life of
it. One has to live in a place to do that. In the
same way, if we only visit God in prayer, as though
we do not belong to Him and live in Him, we
cannot expect to know Him and to find that He is
real. He must be a part of our life all the time
for that to happen.

6. Obstacles along the Way

Having come now to the prayer itself the task is infinitely more difficult. Others can help us with suggestions from their own experience, which may be widely different from our own, and others can help us with encouragement; but the real secret of prayer we have to learn for ourselves. How can anyone teach another person the form of conversation and method of intercourse with a friend? It grows, unfolds, develops of itself: it is intensely personal, the deepest expression of the soul's personal relationship to God. The experience of prayer is incommunicable.

All that we can do for one another is this. The experience of the centuries has shown what difficulties of prayer are common to most people—but not to all: what dangers are generally present—but not always. That experience has found means for meeting those difficulties and overcoming those dangers which are useful to most people—but not to all. I have tried to help people, at their request, many times in my ministry. Sometimes they have come back in a few months, and I have had to tell them that my advice had clearly been wrong in their case. If that is liable to happen when dealing personally with a single individual, it is apparent that the danger of causing confusion is immensely greater when dealing with an unknown reader.

It is important that we should distinguish clearly between the difficulties which are avoidable, the troubles which arise out of our undisciplined selves, on the one hand, and those which are un-avoidable, which arise out of the circumstances of our lives which cannot be altered. The former difficulties have been considered in the previous chapter, and can be dealt with by the remote preparation: the latter are the difficulties which must now be faced.

Here is a difficulty of a particular kind; I quote from B. W. Maturin: "To many persons it seems, when first they begin in earnest the practice of prayer, that the best guide is their own devotion, that in spiritual matters system and rule crush out all spontaneity and life, and that often even the mere attitude of kneeling chills them and makes them formal. They find that they can pray better at work than on their knees, at irregular times of exceptional fervour than at stated times, and that, consequently, the best rule is to pray when they can pray best. Such persons have a proper dread of formalism, and it seems to them as if system and rule must degenerate into formalism if prayers are to be said at stated times whether there is any fervour of spirit or not."[1]

[1] *Some Principles and Practices of the Spiritual Life,* p. 100.

In this point of view there is much that is good. There is the determination that prayer shall be real: there is the fear of formality and of empty custom: and there is the valuable discovery that communion with God can be held at any time, or in any place, (although with the proviso that the person 'feels like it'). Such people can be encouraged to go on with that informal prayer, but it must also be explained to them that the habit holds dangers, for it is a fact of experience that those who pray only in this way generally pray less and less as time goes on. They are using something which is being given to them to help them through the first stages of the spiritual life, a kind of natural fervour and liveliness which, in the physical sphere, belongs to youth but which does not last after it has served its purpose. Those early inspirations and times of fervour become less frequent, and less intense, and, unless with their help and by using them wisely, we discipline and harness them, they almost certainly die away.

Such a person is building the life of prayer on a most unstable foundation, namely, those exceptional times of experienced fervour, whereas the only sure foundation is in the will. And since that is so, more is done for God by system and regularity than those who experience fervour will ever know. For the truth is that it is *between* those times when we experience a warm faith in God that the soul makes most progress. By holding on to God in darkness or dryness, praying as faithfully and as regularly then as at other times, not only is our spiritual life toughened but our knowledge of God is increased and deepened. God can reveal Himself in darkness, and those who only pray in the light lose that special revelation. To guard constantly against formalism must not lead into the morass of having no rule of prayer.

It is when we consider this rule of prayer that we come upon a very obvious instance of a difficulty of prayer over which many people have no control. The circumstances of most people's lives require that they pray when they get up in the morning, and again when they go to bed at night. Many people are not at their best the first thing in the morning, and almost always have a feeling of hurry: nobody who does a good day's work is at his best when going to bed! If some ill-advised person were to say to them, "it is wrong to give God such unpropitious times for prayer: you must really give Him something better than that," it may happen that they cease to pray altogether. People must do the best with the opportunities they have, recognising that they are praying under natural difficulties, and using their goodwill and intelligence to remove those difficulties where possible. It seems that a good many people can acquire the habit of making a part of their night prayer before the evening meal.

Then there is the problem of whether to pray prayers one knows by heart or to have a rule that one will always talk to God in one's own words. The dangers of the former practice are so familiar to everyone that it is unnecessary to describe them. The dangers of the second are not quite so obvious. At first sight it seems clear that one will do better without the use of set prayers but in practice it does not always work out as well as might be hoped. It is not everyone who can express himself readily in words, and the result can be that so much energy and attention is required to find the sentences to say that prayer ceases altogether. And those who do express themselves easily and well in words may be in even worse case, for they may find themselves admiring their own prayers. It is possible that what will prove best—that is, for morning and evening prayers—is a mixture of the two methods, in part using familiar prayers, or reading them from a book, and in part just speaking in our own words.

There is great value, too, in repeating some short phrase of prayer, or just His Holy Name, slowly, with quiet pauses. When Our Lord warned us against "vain repetition" He had not this in mind, but the empty, formal reiteration of some word or phrase so many times, for the sake of having said it so many times. The practice of prayer just mentioned really belongs to the subject of medita-tion, but it can be used with great profit in the devotions of the morning and evening, particularly at the beginning when trying to achieve recollec-tion and worship.

There is also the problem of the way in which the body should be used to help with prayer? It is, of course, important to do this: prayer can be helped or hindered by the position adopted while so engaged. Most Christians are agreed that the kneeling position best expresses what we are all trying to do interiorly. Its very helplessness conveys something to us. It seems to say: "All right, Lord, I know I have been doing a lot which looks like running away from You, but I know that, like the Hound of Heaven, you have been following me. I won't run away any more. Look, I am on my knees, at your mercy." But the fact remains that one can get too comfortable on one's knees—or too uncomfortable. Kneeling is not the only possible position for prayer. In the early days of the Church standing was more general it seems, except in Lent. And standing is still good, particularly if one has got into a bad habit of inattention. To pray in a new position can break that. It is difficult to pray while sitting, and saying all one's prayers in bed is something that only the sick (or the heroic) will do well, for it is hardest of all.

When, however, everything has been done that can be done to make our regular prayer times more fruitful, to replace carelessness with thought and disorderliness with order, there still remain difficulties which arise from our human infirmity. Of these probably the most familiar is that of thoughts which wander. But this difficulty does not only apply to prayer; thoughts wander while listening to a lecture, or to music, they sometimes wander when reading a book. Concentration of attention is not easy, and it becomes more difficult as one gets older, and elderly people may need to be advised to pray for short periods more frequently than has been their habit. It is, in any case, important not to worry unduly about this disability, because it is easy to produce a state of tension by worry, and this can be bad for prayer. To worry may also cause the time of prayer to become a seed bed for scruples, and the growth of scruples is an insidious and dangerous condition. Prayers should never be repeated until one is satisfied that they have been said with due attention. To have 'one more try' is permissible, but not more than one. It is extremely probably that these wandering thoughts occur during other occupations than that of prayer, and the battle to overcome this tiresome habit should be fought over the larger field, with consequent great benefit to the time spent in prayer. If the wandering of the mind at prayer results from a general carelessness in devotion, and even in moral life, this will show itself as the cause of the trouble after very little self-examination, and it will be clear that the problem is not that attention wanders while we pray, but that it has never really been given when we first knelt down.

It was to prevent this inattention that we were taught as children to shut our eyes and to fold our hands for prayer. It is, of course, true that if our eyes are open they may well light on some object which starts a train of thought—as the child's eyes may fall on the biscuit, half-eaten, and lying about the room—but to close the eyes is no real safeguard. All sorts of mental pictures spring to the mind, perhaps of things we have forgotten to do, and attention is distracted. It is a mistake to think that to pray with closed eyes will ensure concentration. To fix our eyes on the right kind of object may help us to keep recollected; the crucifix, or some picture, may provide us with the help we need.

Another difficulty which will inevitably arise is that of dullness in prayer, of boredom, and the first thing to be questioned then is the degree of personal responsibility for this state of affairs. It is wise in this, as in other cases, to look first for physical causes: over-tiredness, ill-health, or some temporary change in circumstance resulting in rush and flurry, are frequent causes. People need to be reminded that a prayer which seems to them lifeless and dull does not necessarily bore God at all. They may be giving Him a service which is as precious and fragrant to Him as the contents of the box of spikenard. There is a sentence in a pamphlet written by Dom Bernard Clements which illustrates this point. Talking of people who feel it must be wrong not to enjoy saying their prayers, he says, "a girl might just as well think that she is thoroughly wicked because, when voluntarily scrubbing out a room for her mother who is tired, she is conscious all the time of not being fond of scrubbing."

There is also the possibility that some new emotional situation has arisen, such as falling in

53

love. This can have symptoms in prayer very similar to those caused by the depression of exhaustion. (It can, of course, have the reverse affect of giving a sense of liveliness to prayer). But the trouble is very likely due to the fact that the person is feeling dull, and, expecting to be bored, and a little resentful of the fact that God does not relieve their boredom, in the same way that if they go to a party expecting to be bored, they undoubtedly will be bored, and are likely to put the blame anywhere but on their own shoulders. There is a suggestion here that might be helpful to some, a method which can be applied to devotions in general, but is particularly relevant to morning and night prayers. The suggestion is that we should learn to think of ourselves, of the person who is praying, in a variety of ways. We all stand in a number of relationships to God. We are, by adoption, His sons or daughters. We are, by His own declaration, the brethren of Jesus Christ. We are also in the relationship of scholar, of disciple, with his Master. We are subjects of His Divine Majesty. We are also His servants. It is a pity to be always the same in our approach to Him, for there is so much to learn out of each aspect of our dependence. Choose which it shall be at the morning prayer, and try to continue with the service appropriate to that relationship throughout the day. It will enrich your understanding, and it should also enliven your prayers.

54

7. The Shape of Prayer

The next thing to be considered is the *shape* of our prayers, by which I mean the order of its activities. Generally speaking, this giving a shape to our prayers, doing things in a certain order, is an important part of that discipline which we find, or shall find, to be essential. This does not mean that every time we pray, when, say, we find ourselves in a church and are moved to do so, we must then think about the order of our devotion, but in the daily exercise of prayer it is clear that there can be good shapes and bad shapes. Our experience with the food of our bodies explains the need of this. Young children, in their innocence, like healthy young animals, can eat anything, in any order, with appetite. They are quite ready to eat candy just before they sit down to eat soup. Belloc's verse about the table habits of the pig who, like us, eats truffles, illustrates this, and ends "Who wrongly thinks it does not matter whether he eats them one by one or all together." Our adult bodies will not stand such rough usage, and find it best to eat in a certain order, and that the generally accepted and accustomed order is the most satisfactory. There is a spiritual analogy. Discipline is necessary in prayer as it is in regard to the appetites. No doubt the saint, like the child, is not dependant on method, order or shape: moreover prayer for him is rather a state than an act; but for us, pre-occupied as we are with ourselves and what we want, some control is needed.

Here then is a suggested outline for prayers made in the evening. There can be little hesitation as to how it will be best to make a beginning. Two words convey its necessary content, recollection and worship. We turn our minds away from their usual preoccupations and keep them steady as we direct them to God. At first we are only thinking of Him, not praying to Him. It is this steady looking towards God which is recollection. For this pur-pose we may well adopt a method we find in the Church's collects. We shall have noticed that they generally begin, not with a bare "O God" but with a relative clause which reminds us of something He has done or of some particular aspect of His Being: "Almighty Father who hast given thine only Son to die for our sins," "O God, who de-clarest thy almighty power chiefly in shewing mercy and pity." In like manner we may find it best to narrow our thought of Him to some wonder of His Being or activity. We hold that thought of Him in our minds for some moments until the recollection of it begins to move us to wonder, love and praise. There is clearly no need here for any prayer we know by heart, or indeed for any words at all. Recollection does not need them anyway; it is possible that worship may do so, but it will not matter if they are rather incoherent or repetitive.

From that worship we shall pass easily and naturally to the next activity, our thanksgiving. For, as we remember thankfully His general mercies while we worship, so we shall express our gratitude for His particular mercies to us—the blessings of the day that is passed. We shall be unaware of most of these since the movements of God on our behalf are so secret, but we shall have noticed some at least and can express our thanks to Him for them. Here inevitably we use our own words.

The third act also arises out of the second and is prepared for by our thanksgiving. In the Gospel we are told how St. Peter behaved when the Lord led the disciples to that astonishing catch of fish after the long, dark night of empty nets. As he looked at the heap of shining bodies he cried to Jesus, "Depart from me; for I am a sinful man, O Lord."[1] The unmerited mercy brought before him all his sins. So we, having thanked God for His loving-kindness during the hours past, are led to self-examination and to contrition. It is when we are most aware of what we owe to Jesus that we are most readily moved to sorrow for the sins of the past day which we recall to mind.

And, since contrition quickens love more readily than anything else, we are able to go on

[1] Lu. 5.8.

57

then to pray for others, for those we already love, for those we ought to love, and for those who pray for us. We shall come back to these intercessions in a few moments.

Lastly we come to ourselves. There is little doubt that prayer made for ourselves *after* those other prayers, will be much more godly than if we had begun—as we are strongly tempted to do, with ourselves and our pre-occupations. We shall be more aware of God's will for us, more desirous that it shall be done by us, more conscious of our utter dependence on Him.

That is a very generally accepted shape for daily prayer—for daily night prayer anyway. It is quite possible that people will have found some other shape which meets their needs, or that they will do so.

We return now to our prayer of intercession. Most of us stand in need of help and of encourage-ment in the performance of this obvious Christian duty: a duty which can teach us so much about loving our neighbor as ourselves.

To pray for other people is a simple kind of prayer. There are times when we all experience the need for the support of their prayers, so that to offer intercession for them is "doing unto them as I would they should do unto me." The prayer we say for people we love seems to us the easiest of all to offer. We do not need to be taught any-thing about this. It is, however, that very ease with which we pray for those we love which reminds us that intercession is not quite as simple an act as it appears to be. It is not only for those of our natural affection for whom we must pray, but also for those we mildly like, for those who irritate us and those who do not like us, and for those who bore us. And besides these individuals there are bodies of people, institutions, causes—and continents—for which we should be praying too. Intercession is, in fact, an exercise of charity rather than of affection. Though that is not indeed its purpose it is the most effective means for growing in charity, just as all prayer is vastly important as a means of maintaining faith. When we find dislike or indifference for a person mounting within us there is nothing which checks this growth and finally kills it as surely as the prayer of intercession offered for them.

It is not uncommon to find people who realise that they should be interceding but whose consciences are always uneasy because, as it seems to them, they do little or nothing about it. That they do much less than they should in this matter is likely enough; that they do nothing is almost certainly not the case. For even the Christian whose daily offering of prayer consists only in the recitation of the Lord's Prayer before he hops into bed has interceded. "Give *us*," he says, "our daily bread; forgive us our trespasses and lead us not into temptation." Almost all do more than that, having a list of people near and dear to them whose names they utter daily to God—a list which they began when they were children and have generally extended since then. And further, every church-going Christian does a good deal more than this, since he joins from time to time in the intercession of common prayer in the services he attends and so has an opportunity to learn to pray for those who are not near and dear to him. We never perform any act of common prayer without some intercession so that we can discharge part of our obligations at these times. We must also be careful with those private intercessions, revising that list of names from time to time and making that prayer a more deliberate exercise in charity by the inclusion of names we do not much want to include.

Any Christian in whose heart the love of God begins to quicken will attempt more than this. But if it becomes a part of our rule of prayer that we set aside time for intercession on behalf of people and objects beyond our immediate circle of responsibility it soon becomes clear that we must devise some system, since it is not possible to remember each day in prayer all these people, both living and departed. If the task is to be manageable it will have to be divided among the days of the week or of the month, as Bishop Andrewes did in his famous *Preces Privatae*. There are small books, such as *Sursum Corda* which provide such systematic intercessions or we may find it best to make our own scheme in a note book. It is also a good habit to remember at our night prayers the people we have chanced to meet during the day—often they will be people whose names even we do not know. The prayer we make for them may be the only prayer that is directly offered for them in all the year.

We may note at this point that in one respect the prayer of intercession differs from other prayers. For it is easy to pray for people while we are going about our business, walking or driving—at any of those times in the day when work is not occupying our minds. Sometimes it is even easier to do this at such moments than it is at the ordinary times of prayer.

It may seem to us at times that our intercessions are so poor and formal that it would make no difference if they were omitted. We must remember then that by this activity we are exercising that priestly office which belongs to the whole of Christ's Church. Through its intercession the Church shares in the prayer of the Lord, the great Intercessor. The Scriptures tell us how, as our High Priest, "holy, guileless undefiled" He ever liveth to make intercession. He is our only Mediator and Advocate. Our feeble prayers are caught up into that great, availing, prayer of His. This is something that He does, therefore it must be something we do. One of the greatest means we have of living in communion with Him is to share in His work.

So far the difficulties we have been consider-

61

ing have been chiefly those connected with time
and energy. We must think now of a spiritual
difficulty—other than the coolness of our hearts
and our lack of zeal for the good of others. It can
be expressed thus. Prayer is communion with God,
thinking of Him, speaking to Him and adoring
Him. That means that we try to occupy the whole
of our minds with Him—to shut out all that distracts
us from Him. It was for this reason that we were
given those early instructions to shut our eyes.
This complete disruption of our ordinary attention
is difficult because it puts so many movements inside us into reverse. But it is not impossible, for
short periods anyway, when it is the prayer of
thanksgiving, or adoration, or even penitence that
we offer, for each of these centres wholly on Him.
It seems impossible, however, when we pray for
ourselves and when we pray for other people. How
can I beg God to help and bless me, without thinking of myself? And when I think of myself my mind
wanders away from Him. And so also when the
prayer is for other people.

It is a real difficulty, but something can be
done to mitigate it at the least. It is largely a question of where we place the people we pray for
and by what path we think of our prayer travelling
when it leaves us.

One way in which it is done is to think of John
and Mary for whom we would intercede as being,
like ourselves, on the level of this earth, as indeed

62

they are if they are still in this life. Our thoughts then go out to them horizontally, as it were. Having thought of them and their needs we lift up our minds to God to make our petition. The difficulty of this method is that it can degenerate so quickly into something not much better than well-wishing or be dissipated by wandering thoughts!

But there is another possible path for our prayer. Again we think of John and Mary in whatsoever place they are at the moment. This time, however, instead of directing our thoughts towards them we begin by directing them straight to God and look at Him, dwelling perhaps on some particular perfection—his unfathomable and inexplicable love, for instance. Then, and only then, do we come to John and Mary. Now, with our hearts full of the charity of God our prayer is no longer as earth-bound. That which we are seeing in Him in our praying may be poured out on them. Our prayer is then much more an expression of God's kind of love.

There is a third possibility—another place in which we can think of them as being. We can imagine them to be, as it were, in the space between ourselves and God. As our eyes turn towards Him, their glance takes in John and Mary on the way. We do not have to turn to right or left to see them and so get them into our prayer. They are within the line of vision of ordinary prayer.

And as God's light and love pour down towards us they pass through them.

Whatever method we employ to help us in the discharge of this duty it is essential that we remember as we pray for them that each of these people is beloved of God. If we love them also our intercession will be strengthened by the recollection that He loves them far more than we do, because we shall want them to respond to that love of His more than anything else. If we do not love them— even perhaps dislike them—the thought of His love of them will help powerfully to drive out, at least for a while, what must otherwise make our prayer so cool and formal.

8. *Practice of the Presence of God*

When we were thinking about purity of intention we were dealing with the remote preparation for prayer, that is to say, with the kind of person we must be trying to be, if we are to approach God. That was the second of Jeremy Taylor's "General Instruments of Holy Living." We come now to the third, to what he calls the practice of the Presence of God.

The Bible begins and ends with a description of people who experience the visible Presence of God Himself and live in simple and immediate communion with Him. The first conversations are brought to an abrupt end by the Fall. Throughout the Christian centuries men and women have longed for and sometimes they have found that first "walking with God in the cool of the day." "Like as the hart panteth after the water brooks, so panteth my soul after thee, O God."[1]

The last book of the Bible describes the peace and serenity and joy of those whose desire has been granted. In the Gospel narratives of the days which follow the Lord's resurrection it seems as though He were trying to lead his disciples gently back into that immediacy of contact, that loving

[1] Ps. 42.1.

familiarity with His presence. His repeated use of their names when He speaks to them would help them to get accustomed to being on "Christian name terms"—a relationship for so long unfamiliar.

That thirst for God of which the Psalmist spoke is a thirst for what people to-day speak of as "real religion" or as "first-hand religion." And what the Psalmist wanted to escape from was "second-hand religion." And the desire is general, the desire to get away from the acceptance of religion and its practice as a formal, ready-made affair, something we do almost without thinking and without cost, impersonal instead of personal, a habit rather than a relationship. Now it is of course very good indeed that we should want this "first-hand religion," but it does not follow from this that nothing else is worth having. It does matter very much indeed that we should have this desire for the experienced nearness of God, that we may have that every hour of our life. But the satisfying of that desire is another matter. It seems clear that it is something which at the best we cannot have all the time. There is a certain ebb and flow in our experience of the things of God, times when God seems very near and very real, and times—perhaps long periods— when He seems far off. There are times when prayer is difficult and it is hard to be disciplined, when it seems that only a second-hand religion is possible for us. That should not worry us over much: our feelings in this matter are not so very important.

We must be ready to fall back on good habits of prayer and penitence.

The truth is that we ought not to dismiss a second-hand formal religion as having no value. Our religion may deserve those epithets and yet bring great blessings on ourselves and on others. For it does help us and other people, if, for instance, we make ourselves kneel down and pray in spite of the fact that it brings us no consolation and seems to be "no good." And in the same way it does help us and others if we make ourselves go to church although we do not feel a bit religious and the service does not seem to make any difference to us. Second-hand religion is not as desirable as first-hand religion, but it is immeasurably better than none at all, and it may often be all that we can manage.

Bearing this in mind we can now turn to consider our task in the practice of the presence of God. The word in general use to describe what we are to seek to achieve is the word "recollection." We may say of someone that they lead a recollected life. They have learnt that they are living their lives under the eyes of God and they deliberately refer whatever question occupies their mind to Him. Instead of producing the usual cliche, "Well what I always say is—," they wait to see if they can hear what He says. St. Francis de Sales used to say that "by the help of interior recollection we take refuge with God, or we draw God to us."

Many of the saints, to help them to maintain this recollection, formed the habit of using repeatedly during the day some one particular phrase of aspiration which served to bring them back to the Lord. Thus St. Bruno used to say to himself many times "O Goodness of God:" St. Francis of Assisi would say "My God and my all:" St. Augustine, "O to love, to die to self, to attain God:" and St. Thomas Aquinas, "Thou art the King of Glory, O Christ, Thou art the everlasting Son of the Father." Another saint compared this habit to breathing; as we draw in the pure fresh air and breathe out that which is exhausted, so we draw God into the soul and breathe out self into the arms of His mercy. It is not a matter of great difficulty to learn the use of these brief ejaculations, thus reminding ourselves often of the wonder of God's Being. It is a habit which can powerfully assist us to be recollected.

It is, however, in our daily humble prayers and especially in the first moments of those acts that the first lessons in recollection have to be learnt. It was indeed in all probability the first thing they told us when someone tried to teach us to pray. They may have said, or we may have read in some book, that we must, to begin with, "put ourselves in the Presence of God" or that we were to remember that we were already in that Presence. They warned us that we must not say a word of prayer until we had done that—that indeed we cannot pray until we have done that but can only "say our prayers" which is widely different.

So we tried to do just that—when we remembered to do so—and we discovered how right they were. For unless we did that our prayer became a meaningless recitation of words or an attempt at a piece of magic, or something to keep our conscience quiet, or, most dangerous of all, a self-communing, a talking to one's self, a converse with one's better self, not a communion with God. However unsuccessful we were in making that initial act of the Presence of God, any prayers that followed it were much less unworthy.

We may be sure that this continual struggle going on in individuals all over the world to take this first step in prayer is greatly prized by God. There is abundant evidence that He cares much more that we should have made the attempt than that we should be very successful in it. The evidence is that the attempt, however unsuccessful, is so greatly rewarded. Even we can notice the difference between one who does this and one who does not.

In such an intimate matter as this it is difficult to make any suggestions which might be of use but there is one point which should be cleared up. When we are told by our mentors to remember that we are in God's Presence the words naturally suggest a spatial approach to reality—the use of our perception of space to help us to attain our end. What we are being advised to do is to bring God, who is of course outside space, into a particular place. We ask ourselves, "Where is God?" and we answer that God is here in this room where I kneel, or in this heart which is going to try to pray, or in that place to which in spirit I have gone that I may find Him. (For we note that when we use this sense of space we still have these alternatives: we can go to Him or remember that He comes to us or that we are indwelt by Him, a veritable temple of the Holy Ghost, so that we retire to what is meant to be His shrine to meet Him).

It is possible that this is the best thing that we can do. But it is not the only thing we can do, nor is it necessarily the best. It may happen that we struggle ineffectively for years using this means and still it remains unreal.

But there is another sense we have besides that of space. There is also *time*. Now of course God is outside time just as He is outside space. "A thou-sand years in thy sight are but as yesterday" and the crucifixion of the Son of God is not far away to Him either in time or space. If for such an end, in view of the limitation of human life, we are allowed to bring Him into space (as indeed He brought Himself) so also we may be allowed to bring Him into time (as again He brought Himself).

Suppose then that when we kneel down and fold our hands in prayer we say to ourselves not "God is here" but "God is now."

A simple illustration may help to explain this point. We are familiar to-day with a new and valuable addition to the corporate life of a people provided by the radio and television. When an

event of national importance occurred a generation
ago the people had to depend on descriptions of it
in the newspaper on the following day. But to-day
they can hear it happening and even see it happening: they can share immediately in what is happening in, say, the White House or Westminster
Abbey. This can be immensely valuable. When we
can know that now, at this very moment, this is
happening we can become a part of the event. (It is
not at all the same thing if we can only hear a
"repeat" of the occasion in a later broadcast. The
"now" has gone from it.) It is the same when someone we love is away from us and something of grave
moment is happening to them—an operation, a
child-birth, an ordination, an important interview.
We want, in spite of our absence, to be as near to
them as possible and we achieve that end by using
our watch. We say "It is 12.40: this or that is now
happening." It is the best we can do: and how much
it helps!

There is clearly such a "now" for our recollection at any moment of the day or night. It was
that "now" those saints we thought of earlier were
using. When St. Thomas Aquinas said in his heart
"Thou art the King of Glory, O Christ": he was
recollecting what is at every moment and is therefore now. No casements are indeed magically opened
for us into heaven so that we can see with our
bodily eyes or hear with our ears what is happening.
But we know by faith something of what is going

71

on. Observe how the Church's greatest hymn of praise, the *Te Deum,* uses this very means among its opening sentences:—"To Thee all Angels cry aloud; the Heavens, and all the Powers therein; To Thee Cherubim and Seraphim *continually* do cry, Holy, Holy, Holy." That is the real now; those are the real praises.

So when we begin to pray we shall do well to remember that common phrase "here and now." There is this alternative: by here or by now, or by using both, we may begin to learn the lesson which the easily distracted children of God do not find easy, to live in the Presence of the All-Holy, or at least to pray in that presence.

We must be prepared to take infinite trouble over this beginning of our prayer. It could happen that a soul in prayer found that his available time was expended or his available strength for attention exhausted, and yet he had got no further than the initial act—no further, we might say, than the words "in the name of the Father and of the Son and of the Holy Ghost." In such a case there is no reason for self-reproach. He has made a real prayer.

Apart from our prayers there are obvious difficulties about recollection. We may well ask how we can continue to be recollected when we are working. We are then bound in conscience to give our whole attention to what we are doing. We cannot indeed divide our attention between God and our work, but there is something else we can do. Thus, a hospital nurse is at work in a ward

72

when the matron enters. Clearly it is her duty to continue concentrating on her work, but she is at the same time aware of the fact that matron is in the room, as school children doing their preparation are aware of the presence of a teacher.

The best known book on this subject is undoubtedly Brother Lawrence's, *Practice of the Presence of God*. It is a classic, but one might hesitate to give it to the young or the immature though it is written with such apparent simplicity. Perhaps he makes it sound too easy and does not sufficiently emphasise the discipline on which it really depends. Finding the practice far more difficult than they supposed they may soon be discouraged and make no further efforts. But they may be taught to provide themselves with some simple apparatus for making a start, such as the practice of a moment of prayer before they start on a piece of work, even though the work is not difficult or has been often performed before.

Here is Jeremy Taylor's summing up of his counsel on this subject. "He walks as in the presence of God that converses with Him in frequent prayer and frequent communion; that runs to Him in all his necessities; that asks counsel of Him in all his doubtings; that opens all his wants to Him; that weeps before Him for his sins; that asks remedy and support for his weakness; that fears Him as a judge; reverences Him as a Lord, obeys Him as a father; and loves Him as a patron."[2]

[2] *Holy Living,* chap. I, sect. 3.

9. Meditation (1)

A chapter on this subject following chapters on prayer might well be taken to imply that meditation is not prayer. It is in fact a method of prayer and everything that has already been said on that subject applies with equal force in the prayer of meditation. It differs from the prayer we have been considering most noticeably in three ways.

(a) The characteristic of this kind of prayer which is likely to catch our attention first is the use that is made in it of the Scriptures. It might indeed be said that meditation is a method of praying the Bible.

(b) We have already noted that in the ordinary exercise of daily prayer it helps us to give it an orderly shape, each part of it bearing some relation to what precedes and follows it. This is emphatically the case with meditation also. Some of the methods of meditation are quite elaborate structures.

(c) In this prayer the imagination, the intelligence and the will are employed more deliberately and extensively than in any other.

We begin with this combination of prayer and Scripture because it helps to explain the great importance attached to meditation by the masters of

74

prayer. People often complain that their faith is weak and vague. Sometimes they even seem to bear a grudge against God because He has not given them more faith. It is fair then to ask them how often and in what way they exercise it; that is to say, practice using their faith. A faith which is not used and exercised can hardly be expected to be strong. In effect one is asking them what they do about prayer, since prayer is a daily exercise of faith. We can hardly avoid being overcome by the secular and the temporal if the realm of the invisible and eternal is never visited, as it is when we pray. Those who complain that God has given more faith to their neighbours than to themselves are failing to realise that faith is an activity and that one of the most valuable ways in which it can be exercised is to pray. And the kind of prayer which is the most valuable for this purpose is meditation.

There is a passage in the Epistle to the Hebrews which explains why this is so. "Faith is the giving substance to things hoped for, the test of things not seen."[1] In religion, as in other matters, what catches our attention most readily is what we want to see: what we want to believe to be true shoulders its way to the front, obscuring all else. But our faith, and the practice of our faith must be founded on what the Scriptures declare to be true, not on what we want to be true. It is precisely this "giving substance" which is sought and can be found in

[1] Heb. 11.1, Revised Version (margin).

75

meditation. The prayerful attention that we give to our Lord, to something He said or did "shows us the Father" as Jesus revealed Him, not as we want Him to be. Indeed, we can say of this form of prayer that it is an obedience to His command "Learn of Me." We are doing just that, studying the Lord's Person so that we may know the likeness of Him we have to imitate and may be incited to do so. For we cannot come to know the Lord unless we try to imitate Him. Like can only be seen by like. And this incitement comes from the wonder and the worship which rises in us as we watch Him at work in the Gospels.

The second characteristic of meditation which strikes anyone who begins to study the subject is the clearly defined structure of this spiritual exercise. It can happen that when beginners, desiring to try to meditate, read one of the numerous books on the subject, they find themselves in some confusion because the directions they find there seem so complicated. This complexity may easily repel them and if they persevere in the attempt they may conclude soon that it is beyond their capacity. The explanation may be that they have read directions written for the use of people spiritually experienced and able to spend a whole hour each day on their meditation. Beginners whose lives are already overly busy will naturally start with something more simple, and may quite probably continue to use it, but they should not easily reject the idea of making

76

this prayer in a certain order, of giving it a particular shape. Neither should they be discouraged by the discovery that they have work to do if they are to succeed.

The third characteristic of this exercise is that we have to use all the intelligence we possess, and our wills, and, if we have any, our imagination.

If we were to try to make a meditation more or less according to the rules and found ourselves discouraged and constrained by what seemed to us too many things to do and to remember, we may well recall the ordinary experience of those who are learning to drive a car. It seems to them at first almost impossibly complicated. There are so many things to be remembered before starting it: so many more when it takes the road: and so many most important things to remember in order to get it to stop in the right place. And they must all be carried out in the right order. At every moment the learner is conscious of what he is doing or thinking of what he must do next. But after a while all that disappears, driving a car becomes one activity, not a series of separate actions. We shall find that something of this kind happens with meditation if we resolutely persevere, though meditation is never as simple as driving a car.

The experience of some centuries seems to show clearly that we normally need a framework on which to build this prayer so that we pass from one form of activity to another. We need not feel

bound to keep to this every day. There are times
when that framework becomes unnecessary because
our prayer moves spontaneously and lovingly
towards God while it is still based on the Scriptures
and our intelligence and will are doing their part.
But there are other days, and these may be very
frequent indeed, when, if we do not stick fairly
closely to the method, our meditation tends to become little more than vaguely religious thinking or
dreaming, and to peter out into nothing particular.

We shall consider this method of meditation
and the order of its parts in the next chapter. Before
coming to that it may be well to say something of
a very simple spiritual exercise which cannot properly be called a meditation but from which we can
learn some valuable lessons in that kind of prayer.
Dr. Kirk has written of the importance of daily
spending "some moments of retirement in reverent
but definite thought about the person, character and
activities of the Lord"[2] as revealed in the Gospels.
Now we want, as far as possible, to make of that
reading something that shall be more than just
thinking about Him as we might think about the
qualities and virtues of some absent friend. We
want to be with Him while we are doing it.

Here, then, is a suggestion as to how that can
be done. You read to yourself slowly a passage from
the Gospels and as you read you make a small
change in the text. Whenever you read something

[2] K. E. Kirk, *Vision of God*, p. 468.

that Jesus said or did you replace the third person
singular of the narrative by the second person.
Thus:—"It came to pass the day after, that you
went into a city called Nain; and many of your
disciples went with you, and much people. Now
when you came nigh to the gate of the city, behold,
there was a dead man carried out, the only son of
his mother, and she was a widow: and much people of the city was with her. And when you saw
her, you had compassion on her." It might well
be that you were led to pause at that point. For it
will have struck you as you were speaking to Him
of what He did that day, that what moved His
heart so deeply was *not* the sight of the dead man
but of the living, desolate mother. You might then
find yourself saying to Him, "No, Lord, of course
you do not pity the dead. You know what lies
beyond those dark curtains. Death must have looked
so different to you"; and you might find that you
had quite a lot to say to Him about that before
you went on. "You said unto her, 'Weep not' and
you came and touched the bier: and they that bare
him stood still. And you said, 'Young man, I say
unto thee, Arise.' And he that was dead sat up,
and began to speak. And you delivered him to his
mother."[3]

That is a very simple exercise. It is so unexact-
ing that it can be done when one is tired out or
at moments unpropitious for other forms of prayer.

[3] Based on Lk. 11-15.

And it is in the great tradition of Christian prayer. First, it is firmly based on the Scriptures: we are looking on God as He has shown Himself to be in the revelation of the Incarnation. And second we are looking on God with wonder, love and praise, talking to Him about Himself instead of talking to Him about ourselves. That does not mean that He does not like us sometimes to talk to Him about ourselves. After all we are "the sons of God." There will always be some exercise of our right to talk to our Father about ourselves. But the founda‑ tion of Christian prayer is the vision of God and the wonder and love with which that vision fills us. It may happen that, after that reading to Jesus of what He has said and done, we are led on to pray for other people and for ourselves, and pray all the harder and better because of what we have just been doing. If that happens then we have already begun to give a shape to our prayer—first that wondering retelling to Him of what He has said and done, and after that, and arising from that, our prayer for others and ourselves. Here are some words from the same passage in Dr. Kirk's great book: "It is only by studying the nature of God as revealed in Jesus—by plunging into the depths of that nature till our alien souls find themselves at home there in the end, and thought moves naturally upon lines akin to those discernible in the thought and speech of Jesus—that we can effectively prepare for the glory that is to be."[4]

[4] *Op cit.* p. 467.

There is one more subject of a general nature which must be considered before we deal with the meditation itself, namely the use of words. There is often some confusion on this point. Meditation, we are told, is mental prayer, not vocal. That seems to suggest that everything must be done, from first to last, inside the mind. Like the ladies and gentlemen in the days of the old "silent" films, we shall have to learn to express ourselves without opening our mouths. And yet the growth of personal religion depends always on the exercise of the right of free speech between God's children and Himself.

Now we have been told often and emphatically by those who live in blessed fellowship with God, that words get in their way: and yet the records of the prayer habits of these holy and humble men of heart show that in actual fact they talk to God a great deal. What is the explanation? The answer is that the difficulty they experience is that of expressing in words what God reveals to them. To translate into the earthly words of our workaday world what is shown to them in prayer is beyond them. If it were possible to do this—and they know it is not— it would certainly impoverish and vulgarise the revelation. To say again to God in *their* words what He has said to them in His, is out of the question. To praise and adore God for His word uttered is the greater part of the prayer of the saints.

But it is important that we look at this question of words or no words as it affects us rather than the saints, because it helps to explain something about meditation. Here then are four observations on prayer which have a bearing on our problem.

1. We may begin by thinking of prayer as being what we say to God. But what do we talk about to God? If prayer is primarily what we say to God about ourselves we must not be surprised if we find it dull, unless we happen to be people who find it stimulating to talk about themselves at some length. We have to talk sometimes to God, for instance, about our failings and sins, but sin is always dull.

2. On the other hand, if prayer is primarily what we say to God about Himself, like the prayer of saints, it will not be dull. But it may easily be heretical. For God is so easily to us what we want Him to be, not what He has shown Himself to be. At best we turn most readily to those aspects of His Being which are most reassuring. It is for this reason that the prayer of speaking to God about Himself should arise out of the Scriptures and be firmly based thereupon. The saints have never said that it gets in their way to pray with His words. In so far then as our prayer is something we say to God, it may be largely what He has already said.

3. But prayer is only half concerned with speaking to God. It should be at least as much concerned with listening to God speaking to us. Here again, though, we must expect this to be often dull. That is not, of course, because He can ever be dull: but our hearing may well be. It is indeed our hardness of hearing that is our great stumbling-

block to advance in this kind of prayer—a prayer
of silence. We are taught to imitate little Samuel,
to listen for what God will say; but can we be
taught to hear it? So we may become discouraged
by the silence.

4. That is not, mercifully, the whole matter.
For it is not only what God *is* saying to which we
are to give our attention. There is also what God
has said. As we have already seen, prayer is, more
than anything else, something that happens in a
Christian when he realises the eternal verities to
be present realities. So it can happen that a Christian prayer can consist mostly in what God has
said already, an apprehension of the Word of God
uttered and an adoring of that utterance. That is
what God will say to us as we wait in silence.

In conclusion then it can be said that it is
natural to use speech even in mental prayer and
that the words will not get in our way at all so
long as we do not have to think how to express
ourselves. Mental prayer does not necessarily imply
more than this, that we do not have to find the
sentences to express our whole prayer. We may
only need to find the briefest phrases or single
words, and these may be repeated at intervals as
St. Francis of Assisi used to do during whole
nights of prayer. A great advantage of speaking
from time to time is that speech is associated in our
minds with being heard. It reminds us that there is
Someone there to hear our prayer.

10. Meditation (2)

There are many methods of making a meditation. The writings of St. Ignatius of Loyola provide no less than five. Such men as St. Francis de Sales and such religious orders as the Oratorians, the Carmelites and the Franciscans have each taught their own method, though the differences between them are often rather in emphasis on particular points than in the shape and order of their prayer. We can derive a great deal of help from their experience. The most important of them are described in Bede Frost's, *Art of Mental Prayer*. Studying these descriptions we can choose the one which seems the best for our own use or make one for ourselves on the pattern which is common to them all.

There is one method which stands rather apart from the others, more simple than they are, admirably easy to understand and to use, its parts so coherent that they are easy to remember. For these reasons it may be found to be the best method when one is beginning to meditate. We owe it to the great French Oratorians of the 17th century. It has only three parts and these have no sub-divisions to complicate them. It goes thus:—(a) The first act may be called Adoration for it is "having Jesus before the eyes." We look and listen to Jesus doing or saying something recorded in the Gospels. Let us suppose, for instance, that before we began our meditation we have read how the Lord "set His face to go up to Jerusalem" to meet His passion and death. We watch Him with the eyes of our mind. As we do so we see more clearly, though still very dimly of course, what must be in His mind; what He has known for so long will come to pass is now very close. His "Father's business" is leading Him to this. More and more we wonder at His devotion, at His resolute obedience. We adore Him for handing Himself over to the Father in His devotion and we keep on adoring Him, in silence or with such words as come to our minds.

(b) The second act of "having Jesus in the heart" is communion with Him. Our prayer has brought us very near to Him: our attention is specially focussed on His utter obedience. There is in ourselves a small, uncertain readiness to obey which has been quickened by our adoration. It is in this and by this that we now seek communion with Him. It has enabled us to see Him; now it is enabling us to know Him. We hold communion with Him in our inmost being, our cool devotion meeting there the warmth of His, so that we implore Him to come to our little souls to kindle them to a like obedience.

(c) The third act of "having Jesus in the hands" is one in which we make a resolution and offer it to Him. We use the grace He has certainly given us in our prayer by doing something. That resolution would fittingly be a promise of obedience in some particular matter, but if nothing of the kind came to mind we could pray for some person or class of person who found obedience dangerously difficult.

Such a simple meditation as that could be made in ten minutes though it would be easier to do in a longer time than that. We pass on now to a form of meditation which is less simple and makes a greater call on our resources. As has been said there is a large number of these methods: what we shall be considering are those points which almost every method has in common.

THE PREPARATION

It is unnecessary to say much about this since we have already considered the vital importance of the *remote* preparation which is provided by our whole way of life. We cannot make Christian prayer if we are like the people in Housman's poem, "There go the careless people who call their souls their own." To be doing all we can to be good Christians at all times is the best—in fact the only—preparation for prayer.

As to the *immediate* preparation, it is the same as should be made before any prayer. "Before thou prayest, prepare thyself." In this case there are three things we specially need and seek from Him. (a) The faith to hold that we are coming to Some- one who greatly desires us to draw near to Him, who loves us beyond our understanding. (b) The humble knowledge of our unworthiness to do so, or, indeed, to receive any blessing from what we are going to do. (c) The desire that is best expressed in such familiar sentences as "Teach me, O Lord, the way of Thy commandments." "O Lord, open Thou mine eyes that they may see the wondrous things of thy law." "Lord, may I learn of Thee."

The Meditation.

Here we turn to the Gospel. It is important, however, that we choose the subject on which we are going to mediate before we make our preparation. To look for a passage after our prayer has begun is an interruption in our recollection from which we may find it hard to recover. And if the meditation is made in the early morning it will probably be found advisable to choose its subject the night before. It is not essential to choose a passage from the Gospel every time we make a meditation. We may instead take one of the great events of the Gospel as our subject, such as the Annunciation or some moment in the Passion or the Resurrection. It is well also to realize that, in choosing our subject, we need not avoid those on which we have already meditated from time to time. A meditation does not necessarily go better because we have never thought and prayed over the passage before. It will often be found that one does better with a familiar theme. If someone has the habit of taking the same walk several times a week he can find new beauties in it each time—differences in

light and shade and emphasis. Whether our meditation is fruitful or not depends much more on the
care we have taken over our preparation than on
the discovery of a subject previously untouched.

The counsel generally given is that we begin
by trying to think of the event we have chosen as
though it were taking place in our presence, in
the very place where we are. We call on our
visual imgaination to help to make it actual. This
is generally good advice, but it is not always so.
The trouble is that for some people the visual
imagination is weak; they *hear* things rather than
see things. If they have to learn something by heart,
for instance, they cannot memorise the look of the
words on the page but they can memorise their
sound. Such people may therefore be needlessly
discouraged if they are led to believe that this form-
ing of the picture is essential.

We think, then, about the event and begin
to ask ourselves questions about it, such as "Who
said that?" "Why did He do that?" "What are the
implications of that statement?" and so forth. We
try to enter into the mind and purposes of each
actor or speaker and to find out, if we can, what
is moving them. There are further questions we
can ask with profit, such as, "What does this teach
me about God?" and "What do I learn from this
about myself?" "What have I done in the past
about this and what must I do now?"

It is at this point in this spiritual exercise that

a real difficulty arises. Up to now we have been praying; but at this point we are imagining and thinking. We cannot reflect and pray at the same time; but we do not want our thinking to be carried on, as it were, apart from God; we do not want to stop praying altogether. We might then find ourselves merely delivering a sort of "pep talk" to ourselves and come to think that the purpose of meditation is self-improvement. To some extent we can get round this difficulty by altering the form of those questions to which I have just referred. Instead of saying to ourselves, "Why did He say that?" we ask, "Why did You say that?" "What are You teaching us here?". In that way even this part of the meditation continues to be a conversation with the Lord. Moreover, when we question Him like that, instead of seeking the answers in ourselves, we shall more readily wait for an answer; we shall listen, instead of cudgelling our brains.

It can happen that people test the value of the meditation they have made by their success in discovering something new at this point—something they have never realized before. This is a mistake. Indeed, when this does occur—when some illuminating thought comes to us—it may even bring its own difficulties with it. We may be so interested in our discovery that we cease to pray altogether. The illustration of the man who takes the same walk daily applies here. Though he makes no notable discovery he has no feeling of sameness. It matters so much that some great truth of the Gospel should be gradually taking a deeper hold on our will, and becoming more and more a part of our inner life. It is not always that new thoughts, or clever ones, or even deeper ones, are needed for our spiritual growth or to persuade us to a more heroic way of life.

This part of the meditation in which we go back to the Gospels and try to take their teaching right down into ourselves helps us to escape an ever present danger. This is the danger of having our spiritual life centered on a so-called mystical picture of Our Lord, a picture not derived from the Gospels, which leaves out His moral appeal and the necessity to try to imitate Him in every way. The strongest and most converting Christians have all drawn their life directly from the Gospels, their Lord is the Lord they have found there.

This reading and thinking about the Scriptures which is the distinctive characteristic of meditation is precisely the point at which we may go astray through not being clear about its purpose. In that simple form of meditation described at the beginning of this chapter the purpose is clear; it is that we may know, love and adore Jesus in Himself. It provides no opportunity for turning our prayer into a means for self-improvement. It is based on the belief that the central act of religion is adoration and that, since it is for this that we are created, we shall of course become better if we do it. Its

90

purpose is not "practical" in the sense in which
that word is generally used, that is to say, we are
not doing this in order to grow in virtue. We must
not lose sight of this truth when we meditate in
the manner we are now considering. Here, also,
what we are to seek is an increase of our vision of
God. What we ask is that, through our thoughtful
and prayerful consideration of our blessed Lord,
His words and actions, that vision, may become
clearer: and as it becomes clearer we shall wonder
and worship more profoundly. The result of such a
vision of Him will be quite certainly that we become
better since it will increase our desire and resolution
to serve Him out of love. But that is a consequence
of what we are doing, not its purpose. I have already
indicated a way in which even our consideration can
be full of worshipping prayer. But besides asking
our questions of Him instead of ourselves, we shall
need to break off our considering from time to time
while we make simple acts of praise and faith, of
love and hope.[1]

There is one small point of some importance
which should be mentioned before we pass on to
the next stage in meditation. Most people have
found that it helps them if they do not use the
Authorised Version of the Bible as the text on
which to meditate. The very familiarity of that
text may cause them to miss the significance of

[1] Note. At the end of this chapter there are some acts
of vocal prayer for use during meditation or any other
time.

what they read. There are other English transla-
tions which can be used for this purpose.

THANKSGIVING AND SELF-OBLATION

When we have done all we can with the
meditation, the next thing is to say "thank you"
to Him "from whom all holy desires, all good
counsels, and all just works do proceed;" and we
must try to do that warmly even when, in our eyes,
we do not seem to have managed at all well, or
to have benefited by our exercise. The advice generally given is that, after our thanksgiving, we
should offer to God ourselves, making our self-
oblation. It seems best and it seems natural, it fits
in right, that, as at last we turn our eyes from the
Gospel, we should need to say, "What reward shall
I give unto the Lord for all the benefits that He
hath done unto me?" What we can do, or can try to
do, is to give ourselves over to God, re-dedicate
our lives to Him to whom, of course, they already
belong. We are moved to do this because we have
in some measure been with Jesus in our meditation,
and to be with Him has this result, that we are
moved to do what He does, namely offer Himself to
the Father. It is His life and His Spirit which makes
our self-oblation an inevitable part of Christian
prayer, and an inevitable part of Christian living.
It can be as though, at a certain point in prayer,
the soul is drawn so close to the Lord that the eternal
activity of His Person begins to work even in the
cold and draughty rooms of our souls, and we find

ourselves holding up our wills to God and saying humbly, "Thy will be done."

That is only a part of the offering that we are to learn to make. Here is a description of this part of our prayer in the writings of St. Peter of Alcantara, the Franciscan: "We offer ourselves to be His servants forever, submitting ourselves wholly and entirely to the Divine Will—And second, we should offer to God the Father all the merits and labours of His dear Son, all the travails of His soul which, in His obedience He endured, from the Manger to Calvary: for all these are our health and our inheritance which He hath bequeathed to us in the New Covenant by which He hath made us heirs of His good treasure."[2] Our meditation can often seem to us to be so poor as to be a waste of time, but if we can manage, even half-heartedly, to make these offerings we shall have achieved something of inestimable value.

Many of those who have written about meditation suggest that, after this offering of ourselves, we should pray awhile for others and for ourselves, asking specially for those graces which have come into our minds during the meditation. Whether this is, for us, a good moment for intercession we can only discover by experience: but that we should pray for ourselves is surely wise. It will remind us of our need and of Him who can alone meet it. And it is good to express here our urgent desire that what we have been doing may bear fruit

[2] *A Golden Treatise of Mental Prayer,* chap. 5.

in us and not be only the performing of a duty to keep our conscience quiet.

THE RESOLUTION

Almost every method of meditation that has been devised suggests that it should end with a resolution. This should not take the form of a vague undertaking to be better: it should be practical, uncomplicated and modest, something which can be done that day, or even at that moment before we rise from our knees. Thus we may resolve to pray to God for some particular grace, or exercise the charity which our prayer may have quickened by an intercession on behalf of someone who dislikes us, or undertake some small act of self-discipline. We cannot every day make life-changing resolutions. Its purpose here is rather to be a reminder that our prayer must affect our actions and to make use at once of the grace we have received.

There is a rich abundance of methods which can be used in meditation, sufficient for our diversity of need, of character, of circumstance. It is possible for everyone to use this prayer in some form and no one should be discouraged because he feels it is too difficult or finds little consolation in it. Its results are too important for it to be dismissed for such reasons. St. Francis de Sales said, "We should come to holy prayer purely and simply to pay our respects and give proof of our fidelity. . . . We must not doubt that such is good prayer: indeed, often of more real value than when we are filled with consolation: yet we may, in such case, make use of vocal prayer, ask our Lord to visit us in our unworthiness and stir up our devotion by outward acts. Or we may have recourse to a book, reading it with attention until we are moved to devotion."[3]

You may be one of those people who have a strong disinclination to use a set form of prayer, a method of prayer, and, of course, there is danger in all apparatus. And yet, I think, there is an even greater danger in despising apparatus. Most people travel further in harness, and they go more directly if they chart the route; though it would be lamentable if they could not travel at all *except* in harness, or would not venture along a path which was strange to them. The greatest saints, as well as the most ordinary Christians, bear testimony to the value of this prayer of meditation. No one should neglect such advice. Let me end with a story. A friend of mine had recently joined a religious community. He told me that he had felt obliged to seek counsel from the Father Superior about his meditation. The rule of the Order is that they spend one hour each day in this way, and an hour is a long time. He was finding it very difficult. The Superior said: "My son, that hour, remember, is *work*. If you will bear that always in mind I think you will find that your difficulties disappear." And, he told me, they did.

[3] From *Introd. to the Devout Life*, Pt. II, chap. 9.

Prayers and Acts

O Saviour of the world, Who by Thy Cross and precious Blood hast redeemed us: save us and help us we humbly beseech Thee, O Lord.

O my God, because Thou art so good, I am very sorry that I have sinned against Thee, and I will not sin again.

Jesu, my Lord, I Thee adore. O make me love Thee more and more.

O my God, I desire to love Thee with all my heart, with all my mind, with all my soul, and with all my strength, because Thou alone art perfectly good and worthy of love. Teach me to love Thee more, and to love my neighbour for Thy sake.

O my God, I believe in Thee, One God in Three Persons, the Father, the Son, and the Holy Spirit; and I believe my Lord came down from heaven and died for me and all the world. My God, I believe; help Thou mine unbelief.

O my God, I hope in Thee, that Thou wilt help me in all my troubles, that Thou wilt strengthen me in all my temptations, that Thou wilt forgive me all my sins, that Thou wilt be with me when I die, that Thou wilt be merciful to me when I am judged. O my God, in Thee have I trusted, let me never be confounded.

Meditation (2)

O my God, I am not mine own but Thine, because Thou hast created me, because Thou hast redeemed me, and because all that is good in me comes from Thee. O God, I desire to give myself to Thee; do Thou grant my heart's desire.

O my God, I give myself to Thee in joy or in sorrow, in sickness or in health, in success or in failure, in time and for eternity. Take me and keep me for Thine own, and make me in all things to do Thy most holy will.

11. *Affective Prayer*

Affective prayer, or the prayer of Christ's lovers, is immensely more difficult to describe than those methods we have been considering. This difficulty arises from the nature of the subject. One can speak about meditation, or discursive prayer as it is sometimes called, because the mind plays a large part in it and the language with which we express our thoughts is fairly adequate for our purpose. Though there is inevitably a good deal that is in-communicable, at least the general pattern of the prayer and its movements can be described. With affective prayer, on the other hand, we are almost as helpless in the matter of communication, of description, as we are in the case of that state of prayer which lies beyond it, the prayer of con-templation.[1]

We can make a beginning by noting that those who give themselves to a life of prayer find that it tends to become simpler the further they go, and by simpler they do not of course mean that it becomes easier, but that it becomes less com-plicated. The analogy between learning to drive a car and learning to pray which we have already used explains in part this increase in simplicity.

[1] See note at end of this chapter.

We had to use our mind and memory when we were learning to drive, just as we use our under-standing and our memory quite consciously and deliberately when we make a meditation. But we do not need to think, not consciously, when we are experienced drivers, and we do not need the help of deliberate considerations when we make affective prayer. There is, in fact, a considering and a use of the understanding, but it is so swift, so momen-tary, that we hardly notice it. "Whereas in mental prayer, careful and deliberate attention had, as it were, to be forced upon Divine realities, and the will moved to act by definite and prolonged reason-ing, in the prayer of simplicity acts follow thought without any appreciable interval.[2] By "acts" the author means interior movements of prayer whether expressed in words or not.

After reading this brief description someone may say, "but this is much better than all that meditation: it sounds exactly what I want." That it is indeed better and that it is much more what we want may well be true, but it is not certain that we can attain it in its fullness and wholesomeness without having first subjected ourselves to the discipline of the far less simple ways of meditation. For one thing, those meditations with their con-scious use of the mind and their training of the will to love only what God loves by constant, prayerful reflection on the word, the acts, the

[2] Bede Frost, *Art of Mental Prayer*, p. 196.

99

Person of Our Lord and Saviour, have been filling us with divine teaching, enriching our understanding, and embedding the things of God more deeply in us. We bring then to prayer a well nourished soul.

But while the soul generally learns to make the prayer of simplicity, affective prayer, with more effect if it has first learned and practised the ways of discursive prayer in meditation, it cannot be said that this order of progress must be observed by all. In one of his conferences on prayer Ronald Knox speaks of the distractions he experienced in using formal Ignatian meditation, and of the encouragement he found in what he describes as "the half-way house between meditation and contemplation." He calls it "The Prayer of Stupidity." "The crucial point we have to decide for ourselves is . . . whether there is a prayer short of (contemplation), making no pretension to extraordinary graces, which does nevertheless by-pass the whole course of formal meditation, not only in its intellectual considerations, but its consciously elicited acts of the will and the affections as well? . . . I believe there is an infra-mystical form of prayer which you can call the prayer of simplicity, as distinct from the prayer of quiet which is the lowest of the mystical states. . . . I must come to God (it seems to me) without any plan or programme in my mind at all, leaving myself in His hands. The will seems to turn to God of itself. I do not know why a human will, belonging to a redeemed soul in a state of grace, should need any extraordinary mystical illumination to make it turn towards God of itself. The mystery is rather that it turns as easily towards creatures. Commonly, at least in a limited experience like mine, the attraction . . . does not last for half an hour continuously: but it is there at least ordinarily reasserting itself at intervals."[3]

"I must come to God without any plan or programme . . . leaving myself in His hands:" the difference between this prayer and meditation is very clear. You look towards God, as it were, and your will instinctively follows your glance and you hold it up to Him with adoration of His Being. In this way we can hope to avoid a familiar difficulty to which Fr. Knox refers later with the words "the more I attend to what I am saying, the less I seem to attend to Him."

While it is clear that Fr. Knox, like many others, found great encouragement through the use of this prayer we should not conclude that it will be best for us not to attempt meditation but adopt this method instead. He himself had evidently struggled with meditation for a long while before he adopted this method and it is possible that, for many people, the discipline of meditation is needed before they pass to affective prayer. It is also pos-

[3] Evelyn Waugh, *Monsignor Ronald Knox* (Boston: Little Brown & Company; London: Chapman & Hall, Ltd), p. 259.

sible that one who has been using affective prayer may need, from time to time, to go back for a while to formal meditation. It so often happens that, in spiritual practices, we need to take some paces back.

"The Prayer of Stupidity" is not of course a fair description of this prayer but it reminds one of the story of the country priest who continually found an elderly farm hand in the church, kneeling very still in prayer for half an hour at a time. He was such a very simple man that the priest was puzzled, wondering how he could fill his time kneeling there before the altar. Finally his curiosity overcame him and he asked, very gently, what he prayed about. The man did not seem at first to know how to answer the question. Finally he said, "Well, sir, I looks at Him and He looks at me." It was only a prayer of stupidity in as much as the mind did not play an essential part: it was the prayer of simplicity.

The second part of that answer, "He looks at me," reminds us that when we pray in this way we can think of ourselves a bit—not ourselves as we are accustomed to think of them, but of ourselves as we are in the sight of God; "dust and ashes" per-haps, but also sons of God and indwelt by Him. The eyes that that man saw resting on him were the eyes of his Heavenly and most loving Father. But primarily he was just turning towards God and as he does so he finds himself drawn towards Him with great strength and sweetness. Bossuet describes it as, "one simple look of ours, one loving attention on our part, towards some Divine object—either God in some of His infinite perfections, or Jesus Christ in some of His mysteries." That also contains an important reminder. We shall need to narrow our attention to some one aspect of the Divine Glory, now turning to Him, say, in His creative activity, now finding ourselves looking into His agonised eyes as He hangs on the cross. But if we come to Him like that, quite simply, He will draw us to Him and our love will go out to Him in repeated acts of reverence, affection and wonder.

It would be a grave mistake to make this prayer sound easy as well as simple. There are of course difficulties and perhaps the chief of them is that, in this prayer, we are in a sense doing nothing— that there are no planned activities in it. This means that we can easily lapse into nothing more than a gentle reverie. Such reveries are so quieting and restful that we may persuade ourselves that they are good prayers, or even that we have discovered the secret of the prayer of quiet. It would be a serious matter to deceive ourselves in this way. It would also be bad for us to keep on worrying as to whether we really were making affective prayer or were simply dreaming away our time.

Here is some advice given by Père Surin for testing ourselves on this point. His first test is that we observe whether our souls are serene and peaceful during the prayer and do not suffer from feeling weary or bored. This can the more easily happen because there is no distinct reflection to hold them and ordinarily the alternative to thinking about something is to let our minds wander, as they do on the borders of sleep. But if we are really looking towards God with love—meeting His eyes—this does not happen. His second test is that, when the prayer is over, we observe whether we come from it with a strong determination to persevere in good. And his third is, that during the day we find that we see clearly how to conduct ourselves—not how to solve every problem but what we must be like, how we must conduct our lives: and further that we have strength in the practice of virtue.

NOTE. I have not attempted to describe the prayer of contemplation. To do so with brevity would almost certainly mislead the reader. It is a subject which needs and deserves a book to itself. Some books are mentioned in the appendix.

12. Spiritual Reading

Jeremy Taylor writes thus about spiritual reading: "Use the advice of some spiritual or other prudent man for the choice of such spiritual books which may be of use and benefit for the edification of thy spirit in the ways of holy living,"[1] and St. Francis de Sales, in *The Devout Life* says, "have always near you some good book of Devotions." It is, however, necessary first of all to consider the importance of this practice—the practice of reading regularly "spiritual books." Some of us can still remember a time when young ladies, as a part of their preparation for life, were taught, rather laboriously, certain accomplishments which were regarded as essential. They were expected to know how to do a little painting, how to play a musical instrument, how to sing a song. It is still possible to obtain instruction in these accomplishments at school, but they have all ceased to be a necessary part of the curriculum; they are extras, and paid for as such by the parents. In the same way spiritual reading, of a kind, used to be regarded as an inevitable part of Christian practice. It may be that people were not taught to do this very intelligently, or that they acquired much skill—hardly as much as

[1] *Holy Living,* chap. IV, sect. 4.

their performance at the piano—but they did it. It was regarded as important and valuable. We can see relics of this practice in the questions still to be found in some forms of self-examination: "Have I read my Bible every day?" (The study of these forms can be most illuminating to us to-day). Such a rule of life was to be found not only among people living sheltered and leisured lives, but among captains in the Merchant Service and people of like responsibilities and labours. They read their portion of the Scriptures, or their chapter of *The Pilgrim's Progress,* or *The Imitation of Christ,* day by day, reverently and thoughtfully. And that practice gave them a stability, and the life of those days a stability, which it lacks now most sorely; and some of the benefits of what they then did is still to be found to-day by our generation which, to a very large extent, treats this means of grace as an extra, like one of those optional subjects on the school bill, only to be used by those with special talents.

Spiritual reading has a very well-defined place among the means which God has given us whereby we may attain our end in life, the perfection which consists in union with Him through love. It is not a casual extra, like playing the harp! It fits into, and has a definite place in, a great system. St. Bernard has a passage which makes this clear. Commenting on the words of the Lord, "Seek, and ye shall find: knock, and it shall be opened to you," he says, that "by spiritual reading we seek God, by meditation we find Him; by prayer we, as it were knock at the door of His heart, and by contemplation we enter upon the sight of His divine glory." And St. Gregory likens the practice to a mirror which God places before our eyes so that, viewing ourselves therein, we may put right what is wrong and make ourselves look our best. As people have to look in the mirror before they enter some social gathering to make sure that their hair is in place, and that there is no smut on their nose, so the Christian turns to his holy books that he may remove defects, and may see the virtues he must ask God to give him.

Or we may consider the necessity for this practice in another way. Our affections and tastes are largely earthly. We want them to be set upon things above, but somehow or other this does not seem to happen in spite of our wanting it. The reason for this is that the blessings to be derived from the delights of this world are obvious: we do not need to make the least effort to learn to desire many of them. The trouble is, however, that in actual experience they so often prove to be not nearly so satisfying as they at first seemed to be, and repetition only stales our taste for them. We become "difficult to please," over-critical, and in the end dissatisfied.

On the other hand, in regard to the things that are of the spirit, the "things above," it is exactly the opposite. We do not find ourselves craving for them inevitably as we do for food and drink. In fact, the things of the spirit may actually appear rather repulsive to our five senses, and to our accustomed tastes. Viewed in the distance they do not attract us, and something other than our senses, and our acquired tastes, must be brought into use and developed if we are to "hunger and thirst after righteousness." We must go quite close to the things of the spirit, touch them and try them, if we are to learn their true nature. As the Psalmist has reminded us, it is no good looking at them from a distance, we must "taste and see that the Lord is good." And the practice of reading about them is the best way of creating and increasing our taste for the things of the Lord. (I had once the experience, when trying to explain this point to a Confirmation class of small boys, of having one of them say, in a surprised tone: "Yes, I see, it is like cheese. I didn't want to try it, but now I like it very much.")

The passage from St. Bernard quoted above also makes clear the trouble, or one of the troubles, of our prayers, and that is that they are so often under-nourished. They are quite simply not getting enough food. A prayer is under-nourished when our concepts remain always the same, when the words God, Salvation, Redeemer, Holy, Forgiveness, and many such, are not increasing in depth and range, and when our understanding of all the things of God has no increase. This is something which a good sermon can do, and must aim to do.

But we cannot ensure that a sermon will be good, and we must therefore learn from reading to ourselves some one of the books of the great men of God, and reading them with prayerful attention. When we have been doing that we find that, as we say "O God," the content of those words is vastly enriched, and we have added to our narrow understanding something from the tremendous experience of the saints. It has nourished our prayer, and our whole life.

Naturally, the first thing to be considered is the reading of the Scriptures for this purpose. It must be remembered that for the laity the reading of the Bible is voluntary; there is no legal obligation on them to do so. For the ministry it is different. Every priest must make a solemn undertaking that he will be "diligent in reading the Scriptures, and in such studies as help to the knowledge of the same." Moreover the recitation of the daily Office entails the reading of a great part of the Old Testament once a year, and the whole of the New Testament. The clergy have a particular difficulty from which the laity do not suffer. The priest may read the Scriptures to himself, as he should do, but he has also the task of preaching, and it therefore happens very easily that, as he reads, he thinks of finding matter for his discourses; that he has no sooner learned something from his study than he is noting it for future use in the pulpit. The Bible must be read not only to ourselves, but for ourselves: any other purpose, for laity or for ministry, must be secondary.

There are great benefits which will accrue to us from this work. First, we shall have that knowledge of God and the ways of God in creation, redemption and sanctification, the methods of His most blessed operations, which are to be found there. Our understanding will be broadened. Second, we shall have a clearer knowledge of what that is which the Apostles speak of as "The Gospel." The studies which help us to the knowledge of the same are certainly not confined to the history of the Jewish church, or the geography of St. Paul's missionary journeys. They include an understanding of what St. Peter meant when he said to the Sanhedrin: "The God of our fathers raised up Jesus, whom ye slew and hanged on a tree. Him hath God exalted with his right hand to be a Prince and a Saviour, for to give repentence to Israel, and forgiveness of sins."[2] Third, we shall have that knowledge of the Lord which will enable us to know His mind about things—otherwise we shall simply not recognize Him when we see Him, as we so often do during our passage through this world. Fourth, we shall have that knowledge which will enable us to apprehend those virtues on which the Scriptures lay stress. As our prayer is being continually fed and enriched by the study of the Bible, our characters come to be formed on it, and that is the character which converts the world.

[2] Acts 5.30-31.

It is, of course, not true to say that this saving knowledge—the knowledge that has in it the power of salvation—comes solely by reading the Scriptures. Generation after generation of Christians have grown up in the past—and in some parts of the world are growing up now—hardly any member of which ever read a word of the Bible in the whole course of their lives, for the inescapable reason that they could not read at all. They were dependent for knowledge upon clergy, teachers, and pictures on the walls of their churches; they were fed, like babies, out of a spoon, with the food that was thought best for them. Even so it may be that many of them knew as much about the Bible as many church-goers to-day. But if we *can* read, then we ought to read, and we shall be held accountable if we do not read.

There are three kinds of books which we may profitably use for spiritual reading. There is first the class of book of which Thomas à Kempis *The Imitation of Christ* is an example; there are also St. Francis de Sales' *Devout Life,* Law's *Serious Call,* Jeremy Taylor's *Holy Living and Holy Dying,* Baker's *Holy Wisdom,* Scupoli's *The Spiritual Combat,* Fr. Benson of Cowley's *Benedictus Dominus,* and Edward Talbot's *Retreat Addresses,* and many others. The list might also include the books the mystics have sometimes left behind them, such as Ruysbroek, Julian of Norwich, St. Teresa of Avila. It is unwise to read without guidance or advice too widely among these books of the mystics, though they have much to teach, and we to learn from them. It is best to look for two or three books which are more easily comprehended, and less easily misunderstood. St. Francis de Sales always went about with a copy of Scupoli's *Spiritual Combat* in his pocket, to read at odd moments, reading it again and again. Such books are excellent for curing spiritual anaemia. They give constant nourishment to prayer.

In the second class of books are those which are systematically instructive. They have been written by teachers and not necessarily by saints, though the Church has had many who were both. Their object is to hand on to us the knowledge which the Church has acquired in the centuries about the method of prayer and the conduct of the spiritual life. Books such as Pere Grou's *How to Pray* should come in this class; Bishop Chandler's *Ara Coeli* (though that is perhaps more concerned with mystical than with ascetic theology); Wilfred Knox's excellent book for beginners, *Meditation and Mental Prayer*. If we want to know how to do something it is reasonable to get hold of a book or of a person who can help. It is, of course, true that we cannot in a sense be taught to pray, but there is a great deal to be learnt which will help to avoid serious mistakes, which will give direction, and which will make the path easier. In this matter it is especially important that reading should be restricted. To read too much about prayer tends to confusion. Search should be made for a book which is readily understood in the first chapter or two (for many books on prayer seem to become incomprehensible beyond that point) and that book should be studied and read again at intervals. In re-reading it something new will be found; the reader will have grown in understanding.

In the third class of books are the lives of the Saints. These would seem to be an obvious source of study, but there is a difficulty. For some reason or other the writing of the life of a saint has been apt to bring out all that is silliest in human nature. There are some magnificent lives of saints; there are many which are deplorably bad. But there is no real difficulty in distinguishing the one from the other. When they are good there is nothing so well calculated to raise our conception of what is possible, to shake our complacency, and to increase our desire for the things of God, and to make us proud of our membership of a family which has such splendid sons and daughters.

NOTE. A brief list of titles will be found at the end of this book which gives some suggestions for reading.

13. Discipline on the Way

Most of what Our Lord teaches us on the subjects we are considering comes under one or other of these three heads—Prayer, Almsgiving and Fasting. These are the means He shewed us by the use of which we were to learn to follow Him and so come to where He is, which is His great desire for us.

At first sight it may appear that all Christians of our day accept His teaching about the necessity of prayer: that some of them discover by experience the immense value of almsgiving; but that, when it comes to fasting they too easily explain this injunction away. Further observation and reflection, however, may well lead us to conclude that there are many who, though casual in their practice of voluntary self-denial, are yet learning the lessons the Lord would teach them through bearing the cross. For those who try to accept the hard circumstances of their lives without self-pity are indeed doing just that.

We shall return to this later, observing only at this point the distinction between the self-denial of our own choosing and those crosses which the Lord chooses for us. It seems best to consider first the reason for the great importance which Our Lord attached to this means for our training. Here are some words of St. John of the Cross which throw some light on this subject. "Many," he says, "from want of knowledge use spiritual goods for the sole satisfaction of the senses, and their spirits remain empty. The soul is in great measure corrupted by sensible sweetness, and draws off all the life-giving waters of grace before they reach the spirit, which is left dry and barren. Scarcely one can be found who is not subject to this tyranny of the senses."[1] He is reminding us that greed does not only shew itself in the matter of our bodily appetites. In the things of the spirit we can be greedy too, continually seeking that "sensible sweetness," apt, for instance, to assess the value of our prayers by their ability to afford it. Even in religion we can go on seeking the things which satisfy us rather than seeking God. Its practice can therefore be fruitless unless we are trying to discipline our senses and to bring our spiritual as well as our bodily appetites under control. Here is another brief and illuminating remark:—"When the wood is green, it must first of all be dried; otherwise you get from it nothing but choking smoke instead of a comforting flame."[2] It is what comes under the heading of fasting, or the more inclusive word mortification, which dries our green wood so that a steadier flame of love for God and man begins to burn in us.

We must not fail, therefore, to pay attention

[1] *The Ascent of Mount Carmel*, Bk. III, 32.
[2] Tissot, *The Interior Life*, p. xix.

to those passages in the Gospels which tell us that we must take up our cross and follow Him, and that in some sort we are to die to ourselves. Such knowledge as we possess of the lives of holy people shows us that they took these commands very seriously indeed. And we do not ourselves turn a deaf ear to them, for we know that when we became His disciples we were called to the fellowship of his suffering. Our trouble is more likely to be a doubt as to whether we are in fact doing anything about this and a deep uncertainty as to what we ought to be doing.

And yet it may be that we know more about this than we think we know and are doing more than we realize. There is, for instance, the matter of our resistance to temptation. It is of course probable that when we urgently want to do something we know to be wrong, some part of our resistance will arise from self-love; we do not want to suffer shame or to spoil the picture we have of ourselves. But just in so far as we are trying to be faithful disciples of the Lord, whom we are learning to love, and to resist this temptation for that reason, we are taking up the cross, we are dying to ourselves. Whenever our thoughts during a temptation turn away from the discomfort of an uneasy conscience towards the pain we should cause Him—or indeed anyone else—there is an increase in us of the interior knowledge of the way of the Cross. In short, to be trying to live always with a pure conscience is to be taking up one's cross daily.

Further, we should expect to find that, if there is something of great importance to be learnt through mortification, God will be providing the opportunities to learn it. It was these lessons we had in mind when we spoke above of those who accept the hard circumstances of life without self-pity. We must not of course suppose that it is only through these hardnesses that God teaches us. He must desire that we learn all He has to teach us through happiness. It is too readily assumed that the will of God for us must be something unpleasant—an assumption not uncommonly found in popular hymns. We might well conclude from the lines

Thy way not mine, O Lord
However dark it be

that misery rather than blessedness is His will for us. But the truth is that we are a part of a world which caused the King's Son to be "a man of sorrows and acquainted with grief" and in suffering learned obedience. We shall have to learn in the same way according to our strength.

There is no lack of opportunity for most of us. There are the ordinary inconveniences, petty hardships and tedium of every day—the tiresome demands of tiresome people, the unnecessary interruptions, the people who waste our time and our temper. Doctors and clergy, and all those whose work is in ministering to the physical or spiritual needs of others, probably suffer more in these ways

than do most people in other professions. Mother-
hood is perhaps the most exacting of all although
it may be limited to only a certain period of life.
All such people have to be readily accessible at all
hours of the day and night, there is no off-duty,
and each has to give full attention and care regard-
less of momentary feelings and exhaustion. Just as
the patient expects the doctor to give his best
advice even though he has been up all night with
another patient, or has a child of his own in grave
sickness, so the parishioner has a right to such
consideration from his priest. So the family also
will demand it from the mother. None of these
can give what is required unless the lesson of mortification of oneself has been learned. We all have
ample opportunity to learn the way of the cross
from the circumstances of our lives if we will learn.

The great bodily mortifications come from our
physical infirmities, from being subject to decay
and to disorders of many kinds, to the impairing
of our senses, to weariness, to mental depression,
to mortal disease, and to the great mortification of
death. Here is a story told of St. Francis de Sales.[3]
When he was in Paris in 1619 one of the nobles
who accompanied the Prince of Savoy became so
ill that the doctors pronounced his recovery hope-
less. He wished the Bishop to visit him in his sickness, and Francis found him bearing his pain with

[3] Camus, *The Spirit of St. Francis de Sales,* Bk. II, chap.
IV, 13. Camus was an intimate friend of St. Francis.

real courage, yet all the while he was fretting over comparatively trifling matters. He was willing to be ill, and to die, he said, but it was hard to die away from home. He wanted his usual doctor, his wife, his children: he was restlessly anxious not to be buried in Paris, and nervously precise about the details of his burial, his epitaph and the like. . . . Next the sick man complained of the air, and the water of Paris, of his doctor and nurses, of his apartments, his bed, of everything in short. He could not die in peace because the hour of death had not found him where he wanted to be. At last he died, having received the Sacraments and submitting himself in a *measure* to God's will. In speaking of this the Bishop said, "It is not enough to accept God's will *generally,* we must accept it in every circumstance and detail. We must not only be ready to be ill, if it pleases God to send sickness, but we must be willing to accept that form of illness, in that place and time, and among those people, which He shall order. The one measure to us must be His most Holy will. Blessed is he who can say from the bottom of his heart 'As Thou wilt and how Thou wilt! I am Thy servant and the son of Thy handmaid: forsake not the work of Thine own Hands.' "

As a contrast to this let me give the story which comes somewhere in the writing of von Hugel. "A good, simple, yet somewhat dry and conventional Roman Catholic priest, a worker for

many years among souls, told me one day in a
north of England town, of a sudden revelation of
heights and depths of holiness that had just envel-
oped and enlarged his head and heart. He had
been called a few nights before to a small pot-house
in the outskirts of this largely fashionable town.
There in a dingy garret lay, stricken down with
sudden double pneumonia, a young Irish woman,
twenty-eight years of age, doomed to die within
an hour or two. A large fringe covered her fore-
head, and all the externals were those of an average
barmaid who had, at a public bar, served half-
tipsy, coarsely joking men for some ten years or
more. And she was still full of physical energy—
of the physical craving for physical existence,—
yet, as soon as she began to pour out her last and
general confession, the priest felt, so he said, a
lively impulse to get up and cast himself on the
ground before her. For there, in her intention, lay
one of those simple, strong, sweet saints of God,
there at his feet. She told how deeply she desired to become as pure as possible for this grand
grace, this glorious privilege, so full of peace—the
grace, the privilege of now abandoning her still
young, vividly pulsing life, of placing it utterly
within the hands of God, of the Christ she loved
so much and who loved her so much more: this
great gift, she humbly felt, would bring the grace
of its full acceptance with it and might enable her
to aid, with God and Christ, the souls she loved

120

so truly, the souls He loved so far more deeply than ever she could love them. And she died soon after in a perfect rapture of joy, in a joy over-flowing, utterly sweetening all the bitter floods of her pain."

St. Francis was looking for the spirit of mortification when he ministered to the dying nobleman and he failed to find it. He knew that God was offering this soul the opportunity to learn how to offer himself into His hands—a lesson he had failed to learn when in normal health. The poor man knew that he must die but he would not accept the unchosen mortifications which accompanied his death. So also we may feel sure that we know what is best for us and what we have a right to expect. We are indeed bound in conscience to keep in good health if we can, and to treat our bodies with the respectful tenderness which we owe to all God's creatures, but we shall fail to learn much that simply must be learnt if we reject always what is rough and accept only the smooth. The means of grace are not closed to us because a heavy cold is making prayer almost impossible. If that were so many people would be without God's help through all the last months of their lives.

What St. Francis failed to find in his nobleman, that parish priest discovered to his surprise in his barmaid, a glad acceptance, even a feeling of privilege, when enduring the hard deprivations of her life. By the daily offering of our whole selves to God for joy or for sorrow, in sickness or in health, in life or in death, it is possible to have a kind of share in the Lord's purifying and redeeming activity.

So far we have considered only the acceptance of these means of mortification which God provides for us. The fact that these are by far the most important does not mean that there is no need for us to make any personal and private rules for mortifying our bodies and our souls. The season of Lent and the Lent rule are obvious instances of such personal choice. If we impose these mortifications on ourselves wisely and after prayer they are immensely valuable. They are shy gestures to God to indicate our understanding of what is needed, and our readiness to co-operate with the Holy Spirit. Indeed, they are more than that, for they play a great part in enabling us to keep in charity with and to accept the disciplines of life which He chooses for us. In such rules we need to include physical austerities: the body should always be given as large a share as possible in all spiritual undertakings. It is recognized that some of the great bodily mortifications of holy men were often excessive and ill-advised, but the Church would have few saints to be proud of if they had not fasted physically as well as spiritually. We must not fail to seek help here for our spiritual growth.

It may be wise at this point to draw attention to a distinction which is of some importance, the distinction between *mortification* on the one hand and *penance* on the other, in particular in the case of the observance of Lent. The difference between the two is that penance looks to the past, mortification to the future. Penance is punishment, and punishment, of course, has to do with the past. The purpose of the Church's observance of Lent is primarily that the Christian family may, for a season each year, do penance corporately; that is, acknowledge its deserts for the grave sins of the Church. It can be also, of course, a season for personal penance for personal failure. It is, in some ways, like the penance that is imposed in sacramental confession. No one supposes that the little penances given after confession, or the observance of the Church's rule about the keeping of Lent, bear any relation to the gravity of sin, or that (as in the criminal courts) 'the punishment fits the crime', so that, when the punishment has been endured, the crime is done away with, and we start with a clean sheet. But it is fitting and health-giving that each year we should, as a family, do something which shows that we know we deserve punishment. It was the Lord Himself who alone could bear the full weight of the penance which sin merited.

It is important that we should understand this teaching about Lent. If the teaching is not received we too readily make what should be a by-product of Lent into its main purpose—an exercise in self-

control which is not specifically Christian, and
which may be undertaken for the unworthy reason
that we don't like not to be master in our own
house. Such an exercise may easily lead rather to
an increase in pride than to a deepening of contrition. This does not mean that we should be
discouraged in any way from making Lent an
occasion for trying hard to grow spiritually, tighten-
ing up our general rule of life, dealing with particular hardness with those things which prevent or
retard such spiritual growth. But the risk that such
penances will be undertaken for self-regarding
motives will be greatly reduced if, in the fore-
front of the mind, is the thought, "I must do
penance with all my brethren."

There is a further point which must be remembered. Acts of self-denial, even of harshness,
express no condemnation of the things which are
being put aside; for the evil is not in the things
sacrificed, it is in the penitent soul itself. All things
created by God, and given to us for our use, are
good. They may have been abused; if so they must
be put aside with a full sense of our own unworthiness to use them rightly. The penitent soul
must feel keenly that the order of God's creation
has been marred, that he has put man in a false
relation to these things, that under their influence
he has sunk and has allowed them to enslave him.
They were designed to raise him to God, but he
has allowed them to drag him down and to blind

him to the things of God. There must be no condemnation of those things which he willingly foregoes; instead the mind must be purified by penitence so that he may see more clearly into the meaning and beauty of those things which he is foregoing, and may appreciate their value.

14. *Staying on the Road:*
A Rule of Life

What we have now to consider is the private rule which each individual Christian makes for himself. There are certain rules which the Church has made which are to be observed by all her children, such as, for instance, the Anglican requirement that all confirmed persons shall receive Holy Communion "at least three times in the year of which Easter be one". But because these rules are for all, they have to be few in number and are necessarily the barest minimum since that alone is possible for some owing to the conditions of their life. One's rule of life then is the private rule which a person makes for himself in addition to that minimum, knowing that he can do more and ought to do so. Thus, many people have their own rule about daily private prayer, on which there is no rule of the Church and about receiving Holy Communion more frequently than three times a year. Many also have a rule about reading their Bible and about almsgiving. It is in fact very general for Christians to have some rules of life of their own.

We turn then to the purpose of this practice and what we are to have in mind when we frame

it. Its general end is that it may help us to overcome our temptations, hold us in the way of holiness and keep us moving along the road which
leads to God. We know very well by now that
these ends can only be achieved by self-discipline:
we cannot keep stedfast in the love of Christ without that. Our rule of life can be an immense help
in achieving this discipline and orderliness of life.
If we imagine that we throw over all such rules
as we have been considering and start performing
those actions only when we feel so inclined, we
realize what the rule is for and what it is doing
for us even though we keep it imperfectly and often
in a perfunctory manner. It is helping to keep us
steady. "The soul that tries to live without rule
never really forms habits of virtue or learns to live
the Christian life as it should: for without rule the
whole conduct of life depends on the whim of the
moment, instead of being regulated with regard
to the will of God: and the soul never knows for
certain what to do next."[1]

There is some wise advice by Père Grou about
regularity in prayer which applies also to the rest
of our rule of life. He points out that while we
should be faithful in our devotional exercises, we
must not be a slave to them. A wise man will
interrupt them, suspend them or even give them up
for a time when any reason of necessity or of
simple charity requires it. It is of course a fact

[1] F. P. Harton, *Elements of the Spiritual Life*, p. 309.

that we must be careful about being too rigid, as though the exact performance of our rule were an end in itself. We may make ourselves be regular because we know our weakness, but not because there is a satisfaction in being regular or because regularity keeps our conscience unvexed by doubts as to whether we are doing our duty. The Gospel makes this danger clear in what it tells us about the Pharisees, and they are also a warning to us of the danger of keeping our rule exactly in order that we may feel superior to people who do not do these things. Such motives make ourselves the centre of what we are doing and that precludes the possibility of spiritual growth. Our rule must be kept in its place, as our servant. If we have these considerations in mind and know the purpose of our rule, we shall not have to worry about its performance becoming so much a matter of habit. Our rule of life is the customary performance of certain actions. Its object is to get us into good habits and such habits can hardly be regarded as a mistake or as dangerous.

Here are some words of counsel by Dr. Kenneth E. Kirk[2] for those who are making or revising their rule. "Communion with God will reveal what rules we need, and nothing else can serve that purpose. It is not by unthinking revival of the laws of other days, but only by wise adaptation of these underlying principles to the needs of to-day,

[2] *The Vision of God,* p. 470.

that the moral upheaval of the modern world and the modern soul can properly be met". Our rule must come out of our life of prayer and it should be definite enough to be written down. It is often wise to seek advice about it from a priest or from some other person whose counsel we value, but only we ourselves know all the circumstances of our life, what is hindering us most and what is most helpful.

There are two small points which it is wise to bear in mind when framing it. The first is that we are clear about what we must try to do each day and also what it will be best to require of ourselves each week or at longer intervals. There are, for instance, many people whose lives are such that Sunday is the only day which affords adequate leisure for certain spiritual exercises. The second is that it is wise to have quite a different rule to keep during holidays. Even a very light rule at such times is better than a vague resolution to do what we feel we can.

If our rule is to help us to grow in grace it is clear that it will need to be revised from time to time. Such revision does not necessarily mean making the rule harder. A sound reason for altering it will be a change in our circumstances; clearly if those circumstances become more difficult in the sense that we have less time or less strength than we had before, then our rule must take account of that. Such changes include alterations in our health and in our age as well as in our work or our home circumstances. But generally when we are moved by the Holy Spirit to revise our rule of life it is because He is moving us to take a further step along our way and we know we shall need to do something to keep that in mind and to help us to make it habitual in us.

In general, the rule should not be fussy or full of meticulous detail for that may easily make us spiritually stale and so defeat its object. It must cover as far as possible one's whole life, since it is the whole of our life we want to put into God's hands. But it must be simple and easy to remember and—most important—it should require only what we can reasonably hope to do in any normal day or week so that it may not often happen that there is reasonable excuse for break-ing it.

We must try not to be easily discouraged or to lose patience with ourselves because we fail so often in this discipline. It is often our pride which keeps us from making promises to God, because we fear failure. And pride can also keep us from renewing promises lest we break them again. Here is a story in *The Imitation of Christ* in which the author for once seems to be writing about himself:—
"When a certain one who often wavered between hope and fear, once overwhelmed with grief, lay prostrate in prayer before an altar in the church, he began to repeat these words within himself: 'Oh, if I did but know that I should persevere'. Presently

he heard within himself an answer from God. 'And if thou didst know this, what woulds't thou do? Do now what thou would'st do then, and thou shalt be secure.'

"And immediately, being consoled and strengthened, he committed himself to the Divine will, and his anxious wavering ceased. And he had no mind any more to search curiously to know what should befall hereafter; but rather studied to enquire what was the acceptable and perfect will of God for the beginning and accomplishing of every good work."[3]

A rule of life which omitted all reference to the use of time would not be at all effective for most people. Jeremy Taylor starts his famous book on *Holy Living* with a chapter on "Care of Our Time." It may seem strange to us that he places this before "Purity of Conscience" and the "Practice of the Presence of God" but the feeling that we need not hurry to turn over a new leaf since there is plenty of time is a real enemy of ours. The Gospels contain grave warnings about this danger.

The use of our time is, then, an important consideration when we are making a rule of life. A great mystic of the fourteenth century wrote, "Pay close attention to time and consider how to spend it, for nothing is more precious than time. In one little moment, as small as may be, heaven may be won or lost."[4] Such care can help us power

[3] Bk. I, 25.
[4] From the *Cloud of Unknowing*, Chap. 4 par. 9. The name of its author is not known.

fully to live in an orderly manner, but it should not be carried to the point of accounting for the use of every minute. Some Christian teachers seem to assume that all idleness is bad, and there is curiously little instruction on the Christian use of leisure in spite of its obvious importance. St. Francis de Sales, we are told, liked to sit and talk with his friends at the end of a meal, and Bishop Camus says that, "When I stayed with him he used to take pains to procure rest and recreation for me. He would go on the Lake of Annecy with me himself or into the pleasant gardens which border its shore."[5] This is very different from that dispraise of idleness which was once fashionable.

The Christian teaching is that, while we are to be careful about our use of time, we are not to allow its passing to worry us. We have somehow to learn to "redeem" time, but there are strong instincts in the natural man which resist the undertaking of that task. The natural young person is prone to squander it, to live as though there were always going to be plenty of it to spare. The natural elderly person worries too much about its passing, having become aware of its quickened pace. Only—sometimes—the elderly seem to achieve a certain detachment and allow time to flow along without losing their serenity. We must seek to achieve detachment in this—a sitting lightly to time's passage—"to be detached in the matter of

[5] Camus, *The Spirit of St. Francis de Sales,* Chap. XI, 1.

length of days" as Ignatius of Loyola put it. That is not a natural virtue: it is supernatural and, in a person of mental and physical vigour, it is a heroic virtue. We have to learn to sit lightly to the passage of time, as we have to learn to do it in the matter of our health and our money and our position. A wise man knows about time, what its meaning is, what kind of importance it has, how it can be used and what its place is in life, and how to keep it in its place. That is not an easy thing to do and sometimes it can be painfully difficult.

That wise man would have the habit of examining himself about this from time to time. He would not, we may suspect, be greatly troubled by the thought of his idle moments although as we have noted there is a tendency to treat idling as though it were the only sin against time of which we must beware. Rather his searching glance will examine his attitude towards the past and the future for he will recognise the presence of dangers there.

Thus, we may think gratefully and affectionately of past days, for memory is a very precious possession; but there are ways of recalling the past, and living in it, which may effectively put us out of charity with our present life and that is gravely wrong. There are people whose lives seem to be governed by the grievances and disappointments of former days, just as there are those who constantly compare the present with the past unfavourably.

And thought about the future, living in the future, has like dangers. Von Hügel, in one of his letters to a niece wrote, "I have now come to feel that there is hardly anything more radically mean and deteriorating than, as it were, sulking through the inevitable and just counting the hours till it passes." To wait for the future to come and take away our present, that is indeed deteriorating and more wasteful than many hours of pleasant idleness. And there are, moreover, people whose lives seem to be controlled by fears or foolish hopes about the future. "What's to come is still unsure," and its uncertainties are even more apparent to the Christian than to others. The Christian can, of course, like other people, foresee events which will probably or certainly befall him, such as pain, bereavement and death, but he knows, as others do not, that the person to whom they will happen will not be the person he is at the moment, his present self. God gives us grace at the moment we need it. The person to whom those hard events will occur will be one who has been prepared by Him for their happening and full of the present grace of the Lord which is at that moment being given to him (but not at an earlier moment) expressly to deal with that happening.

It is the present moment which is being given to us and that moment is the nearest we can get here to experiencing eternity. In it alone we move with a measure of freedom since each moment brings the opportunity for obedience, for gratitude and for doing something for God. And each moment brings the grace of God for the doing of what has to be done and the enduring of what must be endured.

15. Companions along the Way: Common Prayer

It is necessary to explain that we are here using the phrase "common prayer" in the sense in which it is used in the title *The Book of Common Prayer*. We are concerned with the services of the Church and not with the occasions when people come together to pray with one another as at "prayer meetings" for instance. It is important to mark this distinction. In general what we have learnt about private prayer will serve us well at a prayer meeting, but it will not necessarily do so when we are taking our part in the Eucharist or other services of the Church. Indeed one may suspect that a confusion about church-going in which many people live is due to the fact that they are applying to common prayer tests which are only valid for private prayer. The result is that they come to regard common prayer as a difficult and unsatisfying form of private prayer. In their minds, their private devotions are the *real* prayer. They may or they may not like "going to church," but they have been taught that it is something they ought to do in addition to their prayers for reasons which are not very clear to them. It does not seem to have much to do with their end in life if that end is communion with God. So it can happen that the more trouble they take over their private prayers, the more they resent the inescapable disciplines of common prayer. And those disciplines are, from their point of view, formidable. There are its set forms; its cool manner of speaking to God; the necessity of keeping in step with the congregation instead of going at one's own pace; the presence of others so near them and their distracting habits. All these things distract them and prevent them from being quietly with God.

If we turn for help in this difficulty to the great masters of the spiritual life who have written so much about prayer, we find surprisingly little on the subject. One might suppose from their silence that, while they recognise the importance of con-gregational worship in Eucharist and offices, they do not regard such worship as having a part to play in the personal prayer life of the individual. That is, however, very far from being the case. The fact is that they assume that their readers have already this necessary background for their private devotion, that, like the first Christians, they are not "forsaking the assembly of themselves together" but continue in "the breaking of bread and prayer." They have grown up with the knowledge that they are members of a worshipping community—that was the first thing they learnt, the lesson in private prayer coming later. Those masters would say that the first thing to be learnt is who we are—or rather, as the Church Catechism reminds us, what God has made us to be, namely a member of His household, of His family. They would point out that when once we have realised that the really significant fact about us is this membership, we make even our private devotion as conscious members of the Church and not as private individuals.

It is clear that the Church on earth must, from time to time, occupy itself in the way that the Church, triumphant in Heaven, occupies itself, at every moment saying:—"Blessing, and glory, and wisdom, and thanksgiving, and honour, and power, and might, be unto our God for ever and ever."[1] That is the primary purpose of Church services. But our concern here is with the struggle of the individual to be the person God made him to be and he wants to be as clear about the value of common prayer as he is about those he offers in private. It is when he realises the final purpose of God for him that he begins to understand the importance of corporate worship. For we are at school in this world in order to learn how to take our place in the communion of Saints who worship God without reserve. Before each of us lies that beloved community whose animating spirit is God Himself. We do not prepare ourselves for life in that community by studying only how to pray by ourselves. The disciplines of taking part in the

[1] Rev. 7.12.

138

liturgical worship of the Church are a vital part of our training for that consummation. We begin to learn there how to lose ourselves in the fellowship of the Holy Spirit, and that is a lesson we must learn sometime. In fact the purposes of common prayer are bound up with the twofold command the Lord laid on all of us, that we love Him and love our neighbour.

It must at the same time be clear that the effectiveness of our part in this great offering of prayer and praise—the great "work" of the Church —is bound up with the liveliness of our personal spiritual life. As our personal devotions are disciplined, strengthened and enriched by our practice of common prayer, so common prayer itself soon becomes formal, dreary and unsignificant unless our private prayers are being offered with devotion. The Church suffers grave loss when her people are not holding these two activities in balance.

It is in the Eucharist that we receive our most powerful lessons for this training. Here the whole pattern of Christ's salvation is continually presented to us and here we each of us find ourselves functioning as members of His household. We cannot do otherwise than put our prayer into that of our only Mediator and Advocate. We may come to that service with the desire to pray for some particular mercy for ourselves, for someone else or for mankind in general, but this will always be subservient to the intention of the Church in offering this service, which is to take its share in the continual offering which the Lord ever makes of Himself before the throne of his Father in Heaven. There is only one moment in the Eucharist when we cease to speak of ourselves in the plural and that is the moment of receiving the Holy Communion, "the Body of our Lord Jesus Christ, which was given for thee" etc.

What we need to do, therefore, is to apply what we are learning through our common prayer at the Eucharist to our private prayer, instead of trying to apply the experience gained in private prayer to our contribution to the Eucharist. This will mean that we pray at all times as conscious members of Christ's Church and also with the knowledge of our utter dependence on his self-sacrifice for our salvation and with deep thankfulness for his redeeming acts on our behalf.

The other forms of common prayer are the offices of morning and evening prayer. This further provision was made at the Reformation for the public worship of the Church—a provision more congregational and manageable than that which had preceded it.

The Church lays on its ministers a definite obligation in regard to this offering of common prayer. They are generally required not only to conduct that prayer in the public services but to offer it also in private when there is no one available to join in it. It is clear that she attaches great importance to it, therefore. If it were held that the object of the services of the Church is to "help" people this order would be difficult to understand. But it makes sense if it is held that the purpose of a service is to worship God. The priest saying the office alone is carrying on this duty and privilege of the Church, the offering of praise and thanksgiving which is united with the perfect offering of Himself which the Son ever offers to the Father.

For here, too, as in the Eucharist, we learn how to approach God. The words of the familiar Communion hymn are applicable even to these offices:—

Look, Father, look on His anointed face
And only look on us as found in Him.

When we join in them it is well to bear this in mind and before they start we can pray to Him with the declaration that we offer this prayer in union with His prayer and with the same inten-tion with which He offers Himself for our salvation. As his members then we shall come through Him to the Father, our worship springing out of our union with Christ.

The Psalms are the principal element in these offices and it is in the Psalms that we can best learn how to make this prayer. So great is the importance attached to them for this reason, that it is arranged that the whole Psalter shall be recited once every month, which does not happen to any other part of the Scriptures. We should study, therefore, how to use them. It is apparent that it will profit us little if we think of them as having only the meaning they had when they were written. It may be of interest to know, or to guess, what the historical situation was which produced one of these poems, but it is of no spiritual importance. The reason why the Church took over the Psalms from the worship of the Temple and the Synagogue was because it heard in them the voice of the Lord and believed that only after the Incarnation and the Atonement could their meaning really be discovered.

We find that, as we recite the Psalms, we are constantly hearing Him speak. So often the words they put into our mouths are such as we cannot possibly use with sincerity, speaking as ourselves. The sentiments our lips express are such as Christ only could truly say. An obvious instance of this is the long Psalm 119 in which verse after verse expresses the joy of obedience to God's will and the blessedness of accepting His ordering of our life in words which He alone could utter. In other psalms we seem to hear the Eternal Word communing with the Father as in those long nights of prayer, or as the Suffering Servant speaking out of the passion He endured for us.[2] At such times we can only listen and wonder, like the disciples in the

[2] E.g. Psalms 22, 42, 69.

garden overhearing His prayer when they happened to be awake. But generally we can come nearer to Him because He is speaking as the Head of the household of God of which He has made us members or as the King of that city of Jerusalem of which we are citizens,[3] or again as the Second Adam in the new creation in which all members of the Church have a priestly part to play, making its praises of the Creator articulate.[4] Yet again we find Him uniting Himself with our lot in "this miserable and naughty world," praying to the Father to forgive our sins which He is bearing and the scandals of His Church on earth.[5]

As we learn to listen for that voice in these songs of Zion we begin to use them as a means of expressing His thoughts and desires, so that they provide us with a daily lesson in the prayer of union with Christ.

There is another provision which the Church has made to provide her children with a common spiritual life, so that they may each help one another on their journey. This is by her construction of the liturgical year, those ordered commemorations of the way of God with this planet which we observe each year of our lives. As we follow in our worship each twelve months the events of our Lord's life and the salvation which springs from them, the

[3] E.g. Psalms 46, 48.
[4] E.g. Psalms 19, 24, 66, 148.
[5] E.g. Psalms 102, 130.

143

pattern of that divine activity is impressed more firmly on us. We go round and round it, each year a little faster, it will seem, than the year before, as the pace of time increases with the passage of the years. In fact we are rather like the stone in David's sling which he swung round and round, quicker and quicker, and then suddenly released so that it shot out of that narrow circle towards its mark. Just so we shall some time, after following the mysteries of Christ on this earth during our allotted span, shoot out from that circle in which we are confined, released from that round and roundness of time on this earth into that estate of life in which "a thousand years are but as yesterday." The Church's ultimate aim on earth is to direct us towards the vision of God Himself, and the revolutions of the Christian year with its commemorations are to train us for that vision by keeping always before our eyes Him in whom God has been seen on this earth. If time is to be an opportunity of grace this is one of the most important of its uses. It is difficult to exaggerate the benefits we have received from this provision made by the Church. In her intention each time the soul is brought back to the recollection of the Incarnation, the Atonement, the Ascension and Pentecost, it will bring a mind enriched by further experience in the past twelve months, so that we move upwards in circles, as it were, as a spiral does.

16. Destination: Eternity

When we set out on this journey together we
looked for some moments at Bunyan's Pilgrim
standing alone in a landscape without sign posts,
knowing that he must move but not knowing which
way to go. And then Evangelist came and pointed
at the shining light in the far distance. Could he
not see that? And Pilgrim could only say, "I
think I do." In spite of his uncertainty that great
story of tribulation and temptation and faith ends
with his coming to that light and tells how he
crossed the river of death and arrived at the gates
of heavenly Jerusalem.

We ourselves are still on pilgrimage. The end
of our journey is not in this life; but at least as
pilgrims we believe we know in which direction
we should be going, and because Our Lord has
told us so much about the nature of His kingdom,
we know what we must try to be doing now. We
are preparing for the glory that shall be. This
book is an attempt to help with this preparation.

So we began with the task of getting to know
ourselves. Pilgrim started with the question, "What
am I to do?" We start with questions more funda'
mental for their answers provide a foundation.
We ask, "Who am I, and what am I for? Where

am I going and what is the road I must follow if I am to get from my present self to the throne of God?" Such are the first questions, and after them we ask what are the forces which are arrayed against us; what help may be had during that journey and what we can do to obtain that help? And there is a further question which must have an answer, namely, what must we do if we lose our way, or deliberately forsake it, in order to get back to it?

The answers this book has attempted to provide to the later questions in that list have largely been of a practical kind—what one *does* about repentance, for instance, or the sacramental means of grace, or the increase of our faith—in fact the ordinary simple practice of religion. But it must be in the light of our destination that we make use of these practices for that alone gives them their proper significance and makes them wholesome. We must in fact know not only what we are for, but also what the practices of religion are for. To be unsure on that point may easily result in our treating religion as though it were a "thing." Things can be used and manipulated: we can generally make them serve some purpose of our own. But if religion is bound up with the knowledge of who we are and what is our destination then we realise that it is not a thing at all. It is utterly personal. It comes from what the Scriptures describe as "knowing God." It is what we do as a result of that knowledge. We cannot use God or make Him serve our purposes.

"I will tell you plainly:—the greatest and most perfect thing a man may desire to attain to is to come near to God and dwell in union with Him." We come back to those words which I quoted when we were setting out. As Pilgrim journeyed this understanding gripped and supported him more and more. He had begun as such a self-centred creature with something of a whine in his voice, but with each chapter of that moving story he becomes a worshipper, one who forgets about himself and wants only, as every true lover does, to give himself to the Beloved. "To come near to God and dwell in union with Him," that explains why worship becomes so large a part of prayer and thanksgiving mounts in our heart as we receive Holy Communion.

The destined home of man, the place where he is at last to find rest and be "at home" is with God in the eternal. He will be at rest there because he has learnt at last the discipline of dying to himself, keeping nothing back and enabled thus to hand himself over altogether to the Father. We can even in this life learn from the experience of self-offering, of sacrificial love, to know something of what that rest will be. And in this life too we can discover that the more we live for others, the more do we receive the grace which is bestowed on all.

147

"Only the eyes give rest." The poet who wrote that line was thinking no doubt of a familiar fact about our deepest affection. The lover walking to the tryst with his beloved experiences this. Until she is in sight he is restless with expectation. The school boy returning home for the holidays experiences this. He is at rest when home is in sight— the people and the place.

Christians are taught to picture their ultimate objective in terms of sight. What lies before each of us is the vision of God Himself. Our Lord said, "Blessed are the pure in heart, for they shall see God."

Those very human instances we have just thought of afford us just a faint idea of the wonder of that final experience, the Beatific Vision of God Himself. We notice that the poet uses the same word to describe the effect of seeing the person we love as the Church uses in the prayers that are offered for those who have departed this life, "rest eternal grant to him, O Lord." This is not the rest of sleep. It is the rest of those whose eyes behold the unutterable wonder of God Himself in the white radiance of eternity.

A Brief List of Recommended Books

In Chapter 12, "Spiritual Reading", three classifications of books of devotional reading are mentioned. Under the first heading, the writings of the saints, the best known and the most accessible, have been referred to on page 111 as well as throughout the book as a whole.

To the second classification the instructive books by teachers on the Christian life, the following should be added to those already referred to:

Harton, F. P. *Elements of the Spiritual Life.*
Grou, J. N. *Manual for Interior Souls.*
Frost, Bede *The Art of Mental Prayer.*
Northcott, H. W. *The Venture of Prayer.*
Marmion, C. *Christ the Life of the Soul.*
Garrigou-Lagrange, R. *Christian Perfection and Contemplation.*
Underhill, E. *The Mystic Way.*
Also, the 7th and 8th lectures in K. E. Kirk's *The Vision of God* which contain important instruction.

As to the third classification the lives of heroic Christians, a list could only contain the personal preference of its author. The biographies of great Christian men and women are almost always stimulating and cleansing when they are not the work of the hagiographer. In addition to these lives there are sometimes collections of letters written by these people from which we can often obtain a clearer insight into their interior life than from the pages of a biography. Here are a few examples of these valuable books:

Selected Letters of St. Francis de Sales translated by Elizabeth Stopp.

Letters of Direction, Abbé de Tourville.

Letters of Evelyn Underhill edited by Charles Williams.

Letters from Baron von Hügel to his Niece edited by Gwendolin Greene.

The Spiritual Letters of Dom John Chapman.

Index of Names